Pastor
Rodrigues

Developing a

Supernatural

Leadership

12 Key Principles for G12

CESAR CASTELLANOS D.

CESAR CASTELLANOS D. © 2003
Published by G12 Editors
sales@g12bookstore.com

ISBN 1-932285-07-5

Printed in Colombia

INDEX

Chapter 5
SPIRITUAL WARFARE

Who is our enemy? How does he act? His purpose. Who would face him? The cross is a doorway to reconciliation. What does the cross mean? The cross annuls the act of decrees. Breaking oppression. A life of integrity. Helping people to be free. Steps to ministering deliverance.

Chapter 6
HELP THEM WORK IN PARTNERSHIP WITH THE HOLY SPIRIT

Being Guided by the Spirit of God. We should concentrate on developing the vision. Having a close relationship with the Holy Spirit. Knowing the Holy Spirit. Learning to depend on the Holy Spirit. Be careful not to leave the vision. Focusing anew on cell groups. How to build a team with the Holy Spirit. He is a person. Make Him your partner. Depend on His resources. Make Him the technical director of the ministerial team. Renew your mind. Give Him everything. Communion. Recognition

Chapter 7
MOTIVATE THEM TO BE PEOPLE OF PRAYER

Prayer as a lifestyle. Relating to God as your Father. Understanding the Tabernacle's design. Entering the tabernacle. The altar of sacrifice. The power of the cross. The blessing of salvation. The blessing of healing. The blessing of prosperity. The blessing of multiplication. The bronze basin. The five posts. The table of the bread of the covenant. The candle labrum with seven arms. The altar of incense. The holy of holies. The Ark of the Covenant. The Brokenness of Uzzah. The blessing came over Obed-edom. A new pact.

Chapter 8
CREATING LEADERS WHO ARE SURE OF THEMSELVES

A correct self-image. Marked by circumstances. Knowing mercy. The mercy of God transforms. Inheriting the spirit of fear. The spirit of inferiority and fear. Receiving grace. I will give you the land. Economic rest. You will sit at my table. What do you think of yourself? What can you do when there is no hope for living?

Chapter 9
TEACH THEM THAT THEY HAVE INHERITED BLESSING

A watch in the hands of God. The God of Abraham. Heirs of the promises. Decide to walk on the path of faith. Faith rejuvenates us. Vision of the celestial city. He left an inheritance. He saw his descendants. Depending totally on God. The God of Isaac. The God of Jacob. The name determines the destiny. Jacob the man who was worth the birthright. He was worth the blessing. The blessing is much closer than the curse. We are transformed in His presence. Jacob and the government of the twelve.

Chapter 10
FORM DYNAMIC LEADERS

Brokenness. How God treats a leader. Purifying the vision. Try not to take shortcuts. Apply the vision. The fruit of honor. Being faithful in little. The privilege of the call. Progressive development and permanent growth. Have the right attitude. Fruitful branches in the hands of God. Redeeming time. Building a cell wall. Pleasing God. Having a clear image.

Chapter 11
HELP THEM UNDERSTAND THE IMPORTANCE OF FORMING THE G12

A foundation established by God. Finding the missing piece. Record the vision in their hearts. Authority was given to us. Involve the whole church in the victory. Help them to grow. Prepare them for the encounter. The importance of the post encounter. Commit to the school of leaders. What is the purpose of the encounter? The blessing of the substitute.

Chapter 12
TEACH THEM TO ACHIEVE SUCCESS

Common sense. Help your disciples form their groups of twelve. Single-minded Focus. A balanced lifestyle. Homogeneous groups. Working with goals. Diligence in consolidating. Intercession. Rewards. The harvest is waiting.

INTRODUCTION

I believe that the biggest challenge the Church is facing in these last days, is the fulfillment of Jesus´ dream to disciple every nation. This will become a reality if we are able to form every believer into a leader. This means that we need to develop special care for those who are new in the Lord. But the only way to fulfill this task is if we have strong spiritual leaders that know how to move in the realm of faith.

The labor of making disciples is a blessing that God has granted us. As leaders we need to give them the spiritual tools needed in order for them to advance in the ministry.

The first part of the book shares the importance of taking disciples into a supernatural leadership rather than limiting them solely to techniques. Moving in the supernatural is the only way to speak the language of God. The divine riches are only going to be obtained by those who have been able to develop their spiritual nature. God has a world full of blessings ready to place into our hands but He is waiting for those who will stand in the gap and make the decision to extend their hand back to Him, aking hold of blessings and to claim them as their own.

In so doing, they can cause the same thing to happen in others. The language of faith goes hand in hand with visions, dreams and the spoken word. All of this is going to become stronger depending on the level of our relationship with the Holy Spirit of God.

The second part of the book covers the importance of teaching leaders to obtain a well balanced prayer life. In order for them to achieve a successful prayer life they must have an unwounded heart. When the healing begins, curses are broken and blessings are attainable. Likewise, the vision will be understood with much clarity enabling them to begin multiplying themselves.

Jesus promises to equip those whom He has called to follow Him. An architect cannot construct a building if he lacks the necessary resources and likewise, good intentions alone will not get the job done. People who answer God's call to continue His work can count on Him to provide the basic tools that are needed in order to do it.

When the Lord called Joshua to replace Moses, the motivating word He gave him was: "No one will be able to stand up against you all the days of your life. As I was with Moses, so I will be with you; I will never leave you nor forsake you" (Joshua 1:5). I know that these same promises came alive when we decided to assume our ministerial responsibility.

Without God's endorsement, Joshua would have lost power. Without the guidance of the Holy Spirit the church would be a church devoid of power. With the guidance of the Holy Spirit, understanding and speaking the language of faith, our ministerial development will be much more effective.

As Jesus devoted Himself to form His twelve, we need to give of ourselves to the task of forming our people, until they reach spiritual maturity and become multipliers. How would the history be without the influence of the Apostles? Imagine the impact that we can make over the nations of the earth if we are able to reproduce ourselves strategically in others, then they do the same with their disciples.

My prayer is that the Lord will bless you abundantly, and that He will guide you as you apply these 12 principles to your life and ministry.

Chapter 1

TRAIN THEM IN FAITH

"Faith comes from hearing the message, and the message is
heard through the Word of God." Romans 10:17

Rom 10:17

THE LANGUAGE OF FAITH

Everyone who wants to be successful in life should always remain in a high level of faith. Through faith, your relationship with God is strengthened, and you can conquer your dreams.

Faith is above emotions, though it is born in the heart. In general, the human race tends to walk by sight and not by faith. We try to grasp what we see, forgetting that behind the natural world is a whole spiritual realm that we do not see, but it exists because it is real and eternal. Faith relates to us as being of the invisible and eternal world, where the government of God and His celestial court is found. That same faith is what lifts us out of the human context and transports us to the divine glory. It is what enables us to leave our weaknesses and inadequacies at the foot of the Cross in order to clothe ourselves in the invincible strength of the Spirit of God.

Simply put, faith is leaving a world of failure and defeat and moving into the sure streets of success and prosperity. It is to transform the absurd into something logical, the vile and contemptible into something useful and valuable.

If only we would dare to believe, we could open the heavens and cause the glory of God to fall over us and all that we are.

FAITH IS VERY CLOSE TO YOU

"The word is near you; it is in your mouth and in your heart'"
(Romans 10:8).

Many people think they have faith, but the results are completely different. In some people´s lives, faith has only come to their minds but it still has not worked its way down into their hearts.

We should understand that faith is not something intellectual rather spiritual, and it must be received in the spirit.

When we open our hearts with the same purity as a child, the Word of God, which is spirit and life, is able to penetrate the deepest areas of our hearts. We should not pretend to conquer something that belongs to the spirit with our minds because carnal man does not perceive the things of the Spirit of God; "to the carnal man they are craziness, he cannot understand them because they have to be discerned in the spirit" (*1 Corinthians 2:14*).

Repeating a Bible promise continually does not mean that you have faith and can do miracles. The Word of God should renew your way of thinking. Understanding the Word is the beginning of being able to conquer your whole life with faith, and once faith fills your mind, it should go down to your emotions allowing you to eventually commit your will to the revelation that you have received from the Word. When your will is 100% committed, that is when you are ready to develop a life of faith. You can only confess that which you have been able to store in your heart *"Without faith, it is impossible to please God" (Hebrews 11:6).*

FAITH COMES THROUGH THE WORD

Faith leads us to believe things that cannot be scientifically proven, we just believe them. The Bible is the only source that can produce faith in the heart of man. Do you believe that the Bible is the Word of God? If your response is positive, that is a good beginning for someone who wants to start walking down the path of faith, but faith will only come when you have direct and permanent contact with the Word. By persevering in studying the Word, you will be able to hear the voice of God. And when the Word of God comes to your heart, faith is born.

Although none of us have met the holy writers, who were the instruments through which the Bible came to be, we believe what they wrote in the testimony of their lives and what they said about Jesus; that is the beginning of faith.

Faith has some elements that imply the transformation of circumstances. Paul said, *"With the heart, you believe and are justified, but with your mouth you confess and are saved" (Romans 10:10).* Once more the apostle makes us see that what we confess with our lips is the result of all that we have believed in our hearts.

The life of the Lord Jesus was very intimate with the Father as a result of staying in His presence.

He had the voice of authority to such a degree that no one could resist either His words nor the spirit with which He spoke. Nothing in the Universe was able to oppose the authority of His word.

BUILDING UP LIVES

The only way that the truth will last is if it is written in the hearts of believers. How can that be accomplished? Wise teachers who are inspired and used by the Holy Spirit write the eternal truth of the gospel into the hearts of each person who listens to their teaching. Paul said that God used everything that happened in ancient times as a means to bring such teaching to the present day. God takes each experience, each event from past times and uses it to show us His purpose, because the desire of His heart has always been to use our lives to raise up a generation for Himself.

The Lord put this idea in the mouth of the prophet Ezekiel: *"I searched among them for a man who would build up the wall and stand before me in the gap on behalf of the land so I would not have to destroy it, but I did not find one" (Ezekiel 22:30)*. God is looking for those whom He can entrust the desire of His heart so that He can fill them with His Spirit and accomplish His work through them.

By ignoring the power of faith, many leaders have limited themselves to simply giving their disciples a lot of information. Even though the information may be necessary, it may lead to a spiritually unbalanced life. That is why I dare to suggest that anyone who dedicates himself to preparing leaders, should work at teaching and showing them the basic principles of faith. *NEW CONVERTS*

BASIC STEPS TO HAVE FAITH

The whole Bible was written to impart faith to our hearts, and a high level of faith must be maintained. There is one particular passage *(Mark 5:25-34)* that condenses the most important steps in the area of faith. The woman in this story had been suffering from bleeding for twelve years. She had suffered a lot and had spent all that she had on physicians without ever seeing any improvement in her condition. But when she came close to where Jesus was, she came up behind Him through the thickness of a crowd and touched His cloak She was thinking, "If I just touch His clothes, I will be healed" immediately, the bleeding stopped. She felt in her body that she had been healed from that malady.

Realizing that power had gone out from Him, Jesus turned to the crowd and asked, "Who touched my clothes?" His disciples responded, "Lord, you see the crowd pressing in on you, and yet you ask.. who touched me ?" Jesus kept looking around to determine who had reached out to touch His clothes. Then the woman, shaking with fear and knowing what had happened in her, came and threw herself down before Him and told Him the truth. Jesus responded simply, "Daughter, your faith has healed you. Go in peace and be freed from your suffering."

God intervened in a supernatural way. He poured mercy on the life of a woman so that she could be transformed by the power of the Spirit and receive His blessings. The story of this woman is an allegory about the steps that are required to see a miracle.

DARE TO BELIEVE

The first thing to notice about this woman is that she dared to believe. She had been suffering from a permanent agony for a period twelve years. Her bleeding had debilitated her in a great way. But in the middle of her crisis she heard someone talking about Jesus. She knew nothing about Him, but when she saw the atmosphere of the crowd she got interested and began to ask questions about who He was.

"He is the Messiah, the Savior of the world, the Prophet of Israel who was to come," they told her, "The One for whom we have been waiting for so long. He heals the lepers, raises the dead, and frees those who are under the oppression of demons; He is the Son of God."

FAITH COMES BY HEARING

Listening to these things brought hope, and faith arose in this woman, and she opened her heart to receive all of the blessings that flowed from God. Paul said, "Faith comes from hearing and hearing comes from the Word of God" (Romans 10:17). When this woman heard about who Jesus was, a ray of hope began to shine in her life and the picture in her mind began to change. She understood that there was wholeness of life for her. For a long time, she had supported negative attitudes due to the adversity and the emotional conflicts that had touched her life. But she came to a point where she was ready to accept her defeat and expected to die.

That is where she found herself when she heard people talking about Jesus. *Talk about Him*

We also have to allow the Word of God to penetrate our hearts. The Bible is the Word of God, and we activate its power when it comes into our minds clearly, becoming a key that opens the door of hope, so our lives can be restored.

During the years in which I was pastor of small churches, I had accepted a kind of spiritual bleeding into my life. I was winning souls for Christ, but they were coming in through one door and leaving through another. I had become accustomed to living with that situation, but I knew that there had to be something more. I began to seek God so that He would direct my life. The scripture says, "You will seek me and find me when you seek me with all of your heart" (Jeremiah 29:13). Four months after beginning this search, God spoke to me. In the message that He gave me, the Lord renewed my mind completely, making me see that everything is possible through faith; everything is possible if you believe. The key to my hope was to hear the voice of God.

WE CAN HEAR THE VOICE OF GOD

After that experience, I became a new person. And the thing that helped me begin anew was the act of hearing God. The prophet Isaiah said, "He wakens me morning by morning, wakens my ear to listen like one being taught" (Isaiah 50:4). It is so important to learn to listen to the voice of God. This requires that we spend time in His presence, reading His Word. You have to read and not stop until the voice of God speaks into your life. A lot of people read the Bible but never hear the voice of God. The truth is that listening for that voice, through the Word, activates your faith, and then hope can flourish in your heart.

20

If you have disciples, it is critical that you teach them not only to read the Bible but also to hear the voice of God through the Word. God does not just speak to us through the scriptures but also through circumstances, a sickness, a family problem and dreams. The important thing is to hear His voice with clarity in each situation.

Remember that faith only comes through the voice of God. This spoken word of God, as expressed in the Bible and understood through the revelation of the Holy Spirit, is what transforms the impossible into something easy; it renews your mind and nourishes your life, sending you out without fear to conquer that which used to seem impossible to you.

VISUALIZING SUCCESS

Returning to the story in Mark 5, notice that the woman had neither a vision of success nor a vision of prosperity. Her only vision was of failure. Imagine the picture that was in her mind. When she looked at herself in the mirror, she saw her haggard appearance, which was produced by her exhaustion. She felt like she was at the end of her rope without any economic options. Such feelings close the doors of hope. She could only see how chaotic her situation was.

This story illustrates one of the ways that the enemy uses to draw your attention away from God: he often works to get you to focus your eyes on your own circumstances so that you will look for logical solutions, or solutions that exist within your own resources. If at that point, you do not succeed in making progress, an internal conflict arises and you debate between what you should do and what you should not do. As a consequence, all of your attention is focused on the problem and not on the solution. As days progress, the way out seems farther away because it can only be obtained through faith. This faith has been lost because the only pictures that have been painted in the mind are negative, which have closed all doors to hope. Such was the situation of this woman in Mark 5. She had focused so much energy on her problem that there was not one ray of hope in her life.

WE SHOULD PAINT PICTURES

After this woman heard the crowd talking about Jesus, she renewed her mind and began to paint a healthy picture in it. In just one moment, the light of hope began to shine anew, and she began to think about her health at great length.

Once I ran into my nephew´s wife and when I saw her walking with crutches, I asked her what had happened. She told me that she had an accident and lost the cartilage in her knee, which would never again function correctly. Without wasting more time, I encouraged her to paint pictures of health in her mind so that she would see herself completely healed. Once she had that image clear in her mind, I challenged her to bend her knee in an act of faith. At first she wavered a little bit, but then she got stronger in the Lord and maintained the view of the image that she had in her heart. In a matter of seconds, we saw a miracle in her life. She began to jump and run just like she used to. When she returned for her routine checkups, many nurses and doctors gathered around her—so surprised by the miracle that they committed to attend the meetings at our church.

As children of God, we enjoy the privilege of walking the path of faith, but it is important to stop looking at the problem and focus our attention on what God shows us through His Word. If we succeed in capturing the images of God, we will be able to paint beautiful pictures through our imagination and our thoughts, because everything that we manage to see clearly with the eyes of faith will soon become a great reality in our lives.

CONFESS THE MIRACLE

That woman in Mark 5 said to herself, *"If I only touch the edge of his cloak, I will be healed"*. The apostle Paul said, *"For it is with your heart that you believe and are justified, and it is with your mouth that you confess and are saved (Romans 10:10)*. You have to teach your disciples that once they have succeeded in painting their goals in their minds in a clear way, doing it in faith, they should speak about them with absolute certainty as if they have already achieved them. When you write and declare your goals, you immediately bear witness and become totally motivated to move yourself to the same level of faith as your confession.

One of the customs of inventor Thomas A. Edison was to call a press conference and present to them some new invention. He described it with such clarity that he awakened the curiosity of the people. After that, he ran to his laboratory to turn it into a reality. Edison knew the importance of bearing witness and then to work hard for the confessed goals.

For many people, it is very easy to have personal goals and never share them. If they reach the goal, they feel satisfied, but if they do not achieve the goal there is no problem because no one knew about it. If we have an ambitious goal and bear witness to it we feel encouraged to work with more effort and intensity than if we do not declare our objectives.

We should have ambitious goals that imply an effort in faith, goals that go beyond logic. This means that our goals should be conquered in the world of faith. That is where God intervenes and activates His angels in order to help us accomplish them. And in this system of things, everything moves according to the Word: What we say determines what we are going to be. We draw up our path - of life or death - by means of words.

By them we will either be declared just, or we will be condemned. *"But I tell you that men will have to give account on the Day of Judgment for every careless word they have spoken" (Matthew 12:36).*

A GOAL IS A DECLARATION OF FAITH

The Lord always acts in harmony with His Word. Before the creation of the world, the Word already existed, and the Word was with God and the Word was God; He was with God in the beginning (John 1:1). The Word of God created the universe (Genesis 1). When a word leaves the mouth of God, it never returns until the purpose for which it was sent has been completed (Isaiah 55:11).

When a believer takes the Word of God, appropriating and confessing it in faith, God puts the whole angelic realm to work in favor of that person because nothing is impossible for those who have put all their trust in God.

The author of Hebrews maintains, "By faith we understand that the universe was formed at God's command so that what is seen was not made out of what was visible" (Hebrews 11:3). The words of confession by that woman in Mark 5 set the army of heaven to work on her behalf.

MOTIVATE THE TEAM IN THEIR GOALS

When I meet with my team, I ask them for their yearly goals. Invariably, they are accustomed to being much, lower than what I have conceived in my spirit for them. Then I realize that they have not elaborated their goals in the dimension of faith, but in the natural realm. In such situations I begin to minister to them imparting words of faith, encouragement, hope and to show them that they can exceed those goals. After the meeting, we are used to seeing an extraordinary change in their declaration of faith.

When my wife meets with her team, she is surprised to see that she does not need to impart faith to them. Those women have so much faith that they set such ambitious goals that they surprise us. Undoubtedly, that challenge of faith can only come from the Holy Spirit.

WHATEVER YOU CAN BELIEVE
IS WHAT YOU WILL ACHIEVE

The confession of your goals should result from what you have visualized in your heart. It is easy to confess with your lips what you believe in your mind, but it is difficult to confess what you do not believe. You cannot think about a goal of one hundred people if in your mind you only believe in ten. And you cannot confess a goal of one thousand if in your mind you only believe in one hundred.

And you cannot confess a goal of ten thousand people if in your mind you only believe in one thousand. Your vision should be linked to your confession because the confession is the expression of what you have already succeeded in conquering in the spiritual realm. After that, the Lord will move the angelic army so that it works according to those goals. It is as if the Lord moved the army of angels and told them to help turn those declared goals into reality.

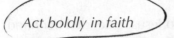

Act boldly in faith

That woman in Mark 5 certainly acted boldly. *"If I just touch His garment,"* she thought, *"I will be healed."* When you get to the point that you believe, visualize, and confess, then it is time to go to work. And in this process, you cannot let yourself be hindered by obstacles and adversity. That woman knew that it was almost impossible to get to Jesus, but as she followed the correct steps, her vision prompted her to remove all the obstacles that were in her way and press on until she reached Jesus. The culmination of things depended on your actions. If she had waited for Jesus to be detained and returned to where she was, she probably would not have experienced that miracle in her body.

Faith to overcome obstacles

Unfortunately, not everyone is as motivated as that woman was. Many people develop an attitude of complaining.

They believe that they are not important, that God has forgotten their needs. They feel that if they were important to Him, He would have already done something to help. But this woman was very determined. Her thought process must have been, "If Jesus is not coming to me, then I'm going to go to Him. The obstacles in my way don't matter to me." Jesus took into account this woman's act of faith because she had taken the correct steps to experience the power of God in her life.

The woman made her way to Jesus, extended her hand, and touched the edge of his garment. When she did that, she was immediately healed. When you open up the way to get to God in the midst of adversity and press into His presence, you can make things happen. Faith is what forges your destiny because it produces so much desire inside of you to take action. Faith sets you so high in the spiritual realm that it does not permit you to see obstacles. Faith carries you into Jesus' presence, not just to touch Him but to extract the power of God in your favor. That is why Jesus praised this woman's action: "Daughter, your faith has healed you. Go in peace and be freed from your suffering."(Mark 5:34).

Faith like a child

Jesus told us that unless we become like little children, we would not enter into the kingdom of God. To His accusers, who criticized Him for allowing the children to continue in raucous praise to Him, He said *"Have you never read; 'Out of the mouths of babes and infants you have obtained perfect praise'." Psalms 8:2*

I learnt one of the greatest lessons of faith from one of my daughters. When my daughter, Sara, was five years old, she had a great desire to buy a motorcycle that she saw in one of the stores in Bogotá. One day, she took me to that shopping center and told me, "Daddy, I want to buy this motorcycle." When I saw the price ($800!) I told her, "Sweetheart, that is a very expensive toy, and I am not going to buy it for you."

My daughter did not argue. We went to the store next door. "Daddy," she said, "Will you buy me this purse ?"

"Of course, sweetheart," I answered. The price was very reasonable, so I bought it for her.

Later, she asked me, "Daddy, can you give me ten dollars?"

"Sure," I said, and I gave her the ten dollars.

She immediately looked at me and said, "Starting right now, I'm going to save the money to buy my motorcycle in one week". My daughter is very fearless and decisive, but I thought she was talking about something that she could not conquer. Later, I understood that, for her, it was like a challenge of faith.

That same day, she went to her grandparent's house and to the houses of each of her uncles and asked each of them for ten dollars. Later, she went to a meeting for youth leaders and repeated the process. She did the same thing at the men's meeting and the women's meeting.

With that boldness that characterizes her, she had gathered more than eight hundred dollars within a week. Then she put the money in my hand and said to me, "Daddy, I got the money so I can buy the motorcycle."

When I received the money, I told her, "Sara, you are a woman of faith. You can conquer whatever you want in this life. By gathering this money you have demonstrated that there are no obstacles or barriers for you."

God always permits challenges in your life. Maybe at the beginning you see them as very high mountains that you have to climb. However when you succeed in getting to the top, you realize that the mountain was not really that high and that there are other mountains that are much bigger. A challenge that has been conquered will motivate you to go after others that are even greater. That is why it is essential to have challenges of faith within your team. When your members feel the satisfaction of having conquered something, they will be filled with enthusiasm to confront any situation that you have to conquer.

Chapter 2

HAVE VISIONARY LEADERS

Mark 10:46-52,12:3

RECOVERING THE VISION

Have you ever had the chance to see someone who's sight had been recovered after having been blind for many years ? I have been able to see that in several of our healing services. They cannot stop crying in gratitude to God. This miracle was something that not only they, but their families were hoping and longing for.

I remember that in one of those meetings, the sick people had come to the front. When I was asking for testimonies, a lady came up with a girl who was about ten years old. She had the girl in her arms and began telling me, "My daughter can see; she was blind, and now she sees." At that moment, I thought she was exaggerating, and I did not give much weight to what she was saying. I turned my attention to other miracles that were happening. Later, I kept looking at the girl, as she stared back at me. I waved a greeting to her, and she did the same to me. I quickly called her to the platform and asked her mother what sickness the girl had. She told me, "Since she was born, she had problems with her eyes and had lost her vision, leaving her practically blind, but just now when we were praying my daughter began to see." Imagine the reaction of those who were present in the auditorium! They all celebrated the miracle of sight that this precious child had received.

Think for a moment about what happens in the spiritual world where millions of angels are observing you. Maybe you were born into the ministry with little vision and with the passing of years you ended up loosing your sight completely. Suddenly, you decide to believe God, and He gives your sight back; your spiritual eyes open. Now you can see and understand everything clearly. How would the angels in heaven celebrate this great miracle?

WITHOUT VISION THE WAY IS NOT CLEARED

Jesus performed one of the greatest miracles of healing when he gave back to Bartimaeus his ability to see, (*Mark 10:52*.) This miracle becomes a prototype for those who have not been able to see the wonders of the spiritual world because even though they have eyes, their eyes have remained closed. We should follow Bartimaeus' example and defy our circumstances in order to receive that great miracle and have our eyes opened.

A story that I heard a preacher tell many years ago, grabbed my attention. He was talking about a man who wanted to do an experiment with some blind men, so he took four of them and put them around an elephant. Although none of them knew what was in front of them, each one of them was asked to describe their perception of what they touched. So the first blind man reached out to touch one of the legs, which he described as a column. The second blind man reached out to touch the elephant's belly, which he described as a wall. The third blind man reached out to touch its tail, which he guessed was a broom. Finally, the fourth blind man reached out to touch one of the elephant's tusks, which he declared to be a dagger.

What do we learn from this story? We learn that we will never describe things around us correctly if we do not have vision.

Many of the pastors who visit us in Bogota with the desire to learn about the "vision" go searching for a method; they want a mathematical formula; a way to do things in a mechanical way. Although methods generally help, the most important thing is vision. A blind man can have all kinds of instructions when he wants to move from one place to another, but he is always going to have problems in the road that he would otherwise be able to avoid if he could only see. In the same way, although every step of the vision may be very clear in someone's mind, this will not be of much help if his spiritual eyes have still not been opened. I know that for some people, having a group of twelve makes them think that they are in the "vision". Others may say, "The Vision is to form cell groups." There may still be others who are sure that the vision is to work with homogeneous groups. Others might assert that the vision is based on spiritual warfare. Although each person may accurately describe a part of the vision, it must be considered as a whole entity. The ability to integrate each of the individual elements into a complete vision is what enables leaders to succeed.

WITHOUT VISION, YOU CANNOT DISTINGUISH THINGS AS THEY REALLY ARE

Bartimaeus lived near Jericho. We know that Jericho was a cursed city. After conquering it, Joshua said, "Cursed before the LORD is the man who undertakes to rebuild this city, Jericho" (Joshua 6:26).

Since that time, talking about this city is like talking about a curse. Due to lack of vision, this man could not distinguish between what was beautiful and what was ugly, between a blessing and a curse, between prosperity and poverty. For a blind man, his world is what surrounds him. Only that which he can touch; his development as a person is generally very limited.

Solomon said, "_Without vision, the people perish_".

WITHOUT VISION, YOU DEPEND
ON GOD'S MERCY

Bartimaeus was sitting next to the road, begging, as his custom was. This man can represent a ministry that has lost its vision and has developed a passive attitude because when you lose the vision you also lose the desire to win souls. It depends on the preacher to keep the ministry alive.

The gospel that Jesus preached was complete He always worried about the needs of the people. With that motivation, He lived a life of healing the sick, cleansing lepers, forgiving sinners, and giving hope to the homeless. Loss of vision is the result of the strategy that the devil uses to take us out of combat; his goal is to knock leaders down and take away their desire to conquer.

WITHOUT VISION, YOU ARE OUTSIDE
OF HIS PURPOSE

This blind man was beside the road. There is a big difference between being "beside the road" and being "on the road." Jesus said, "*I am the way*" being next to the road means that because of his blindness, he felt powerless to move himself from one place to another.

When a believer succeeds in entering into an intimate relationship with Jesus through a life of prayer - which is the only way you can stay on the road - this relationship opens your eyes to see His light clearly. Your spirit is lifted up and you feel that you are one with Him. Your mind opens, and you understand with clarity the revelation of His Word. Whoever is not on the road will not be able to see the glory of the Lord's unveiled face, as in a mirror (*2 Corinthians 3:18*).

CRYING OUT FOR MERCY

JR 33:3

When Bartimaeus knew that Jesus was passing by that place, he cried out, asking for mercy.

The Lord said, *"Cry out to me and I will answer you and tell you great and unsearchable things that you do not know" (Jeremiah 33:3).* Even though the people that were around Bartimaeus tried to get him to keep quiet, implying that he should simply accept the situation, he did not let the opposition intimidate him. Instead, he cried out to Jesus even louder, "Jesus, son of David, be merciful to me."

We should understand that perseverance is a fundamental requirement in order to receive a miracle, of our vision being restored. The opposition of the people did not matter much to this man, and neither was the contempt that some of them showed for him. On the contrary, he raised his voice even more and implored Jesus for mercy as loud as he could. And the Lord heard the blind man's cry. Jesus stopped and sent someone to get him.

If this man had not cried out with all of his heart and all of his strength, he never would have received the miracle. Many times, God lets us get into desperate situations so that we take refuge in prayer and cry out until we receive His response.

STEPS TO RECOVERING VISION

A messenger whom Jesus sent, told Bartimaeus, "Be encouraged and get up, He's calling you." Think for a moment about what those three phrases mean.

Be encouraged

The response of this blind man could have been different. For someone who has lost his family, his friends, money, respect, even his desire to live, it is not easy to be encouraged. Sadly, many ministers who have experienced ministerial sterility for many years begin to believe that it is not worth the trouble to keep trying. For them, it becomes difficult to believe that God can use them as instruments of power in His hands and experience explosive growth within their congregations.

Such pastors are not encouraged to try new methods. In order to see miracles in the ministry, we need to take new strength. Desire gives new hope to our souls: We must believe that the miracle of being in the vision will enable us to be conquerors with Him.

Get up

Adversity leaves many people defeated. Remember when Moses heard the armies of Pharaoh approaching? They were riding furiously against the Israelites, and Moses threw himself down on the ground and cried out to God for protection. The Lord responded, "Why are you crying out to me? Tell the people to march" (Exodus 14:15). God told the patriarch, Job, who was prostrate in his great tribulation, to get up and pray for his enemies so that his affliction would be removed. The prodigal son was inspired to get up and go to his father saying, "Father, I have sinned against heaven and against you" (Luke 15:21).

In each of these situations, the people had to make an effort; they had to get up from a situation, before God would bless them. I know that many leaders make a great effort to attend the different conventions that we have organized in different places around the world in order to teach the vision; with that effort, they are demonstrating that they want the miracle to happen in their ministries as soon as possible.

Hear the voice of the Lord calling you

You cannot approach God if He does not first call you. The fact that you are reading this book right now is a sign that God is interested in your life and ministry. He is inviting you to take a deep breath and to get up with the firm decision to obey His call. You should understand that you are God's answer to meet the spiritual needs of this world in these days and He can, fill the void in many hearts through the vision.

Act in faith

Bartimaeus threw off his coat, got up and went to Jesus. The coat was a sign that marked him as a blind person. The simple act of throwing off this coat was an act of faith. He was sure that he would no longer need it. In response to the call of Jesus and with conviction he thought, "If He's calling me it's because He's going to heal me and I will not have to use this cape any more because I will regain my sight." It is so important to cast off those ideas that limit us in the development of our ministry and to be completely sure, that God will work a miracle in our lives by opening our spiritual eyes so that the vision becomes part of our everyday existence, to the point where our actions are the same as Jesus' when He walked on this earth.

Desire the vision

"What do you want me to do for you?" This same question was not only for Bartimaeus but it is also for you today. Think for a minute. The author of life, the owner of everything that exists - all the riches of the earth - the one and only sovereign God of the universe who has whatever you need, places Himself at your disposal and asks you, "What can I do for you?" Even though Bartimaeus had many needs in his daily life and could have asked for help in restoring his family or his finances, he had only one burning desire in his heart: that the Lord would give him vision.

If you have vision, everything else will work itself out (Matthew 6:33). Unfortunately, most of us ask God for everything except vision. When God told Solomon that he could ask for anything that he wanted, he could have asked for riches or that the Lord would avenge the wrongs of his enemies, but he did not.

Solomon asked for wisdom and understanding to know how to govern rightly (1 Kings 3:9). Solomon's request pleased God so much that He not only gave Solomon wisdom to govern, but riches as well. Wisdom consists of understanding the heart of God, as revealed through His Word, and being ready to obey Him in everything.

WHAT WE SEE IN THE SPIRITUAL IS REPRODUCED IN THE NATURAL

When we enter into the life of the Spirit, we can say that we have entered into the world of God. He opens our spiritual eyes and allows us to see with clarity what He has for us because what we need to see is not in the natural realm; it is only in the spiritual realm. The human eye will never be able to see what God wants us to see, but when we enter into the dimension of faith, the Spirit begins to bring clear images into our lives and into our minds.

He feeds us and motivates us to be conquerors. That is why when we dream, it feels like we are present in the dream, when we enter God's world the same thing happens and we begin to receive His dreams. It is very real.

When Joseph dreamed about the eleven sheaves that bowed down to him or the eleven stars that bowed down to him with the son and moon (Genesis 37:7), God was showing him something that human logic could not accept; it was odd that the youngest of the brothers would dream of being over the older ones.

When God gives us visions, they are often seen as a contradiction to logic and we can find people who will try to tell us, "What is this that you are dreaming? Do not keep dreaming like that, that is absurd. Do not accept that dream."

We should know that every dream that comes from the Spirit always motivates us to protect our lives, care for our families, and expand the Kingdom of God. The only way to have God's dreams is if the Spirit brings His revelation into our lives, and this is something that only occurs because our spirits are united with the Spirit of God.

It is not by human effort or human power, it is only by the unity of our spirits with His divine presence.

41

MY MINISTRY CHANGED WHEN I WAS ABLE TO SEE

When God spoke to me in 1983 and told me to dream of a big church; my spiritual eyes were immediately opened and I appropriated that word. I could see the multitudes appear so clearly as the sand on a beach. That vision changed my life completely. Before that moment, it was very difficult for me to see salvation of souls, but since He opened my eyes I have continuously seen thousands and thousands of people receive salvation and become Christians. I have seen the Holy Spirit heal many bodies.

I can tell you that there is a big difference between those who see and those who are ministerially blind. Maybe when you became a Christian you had vision, but circumstances gradually turned your focus away from it. If so, right now, today, ask God in prayer: *"Lord, be merciful to me, and help me recover my vision. Help me to understand your purpose for my life. Help me to understand that your vision is the most important part of my life. I want to recover it in order to be able to fulfill your purpose for my life".*

The Lord told Bartimaeus that it would happen with him according to his faith. Immediately he regained his sight and followed Jesus on the road. He no longer wanted to be along the side of the road. He moved into the street, entered the vision, and followed Jesus on the road.

Now, doing the vision is very easy.

In this very moment, it is important that you stop reading this book and cry out to God with all of your strength, just as Bartimaeus did. Ask Jesus to be merciful to you and to give you vision. Keep crying out until you feel that the miracle has become a reality in your life.

Chapter 3

HELP THEM CONQUER THEIR DREAMS

"And Joseph had a dream..."

Genesis 37:5

HELPING YOUR DISCIPLES

Each person that God places on a team needs words of encouragement and motivation. You, as the leader, should help others keep their dreams alive and feed them daily so that they do not lose the vision and the objective that the Lord has given them. How? Simply invest in them whatever time is necessary in order to help them overcome their emotional conflicts.

The great majority of human beings have dreams that never become reality because they throw in the towel too soon. They allow their character to crack under pressure, and they give up in the middle of the test. The circumstances that Joseph endured in his personal life serve as an example to guide us in helping our disciples overcome, and to keep moving forward in the middle of their struggles so that they can make their dreams come true.

VERY FEW PEOPLE UNDERSTAND A DREAMER

God gave Joseph a dream that showed the path that his life would take and the grand challenges that God had for him. When Joseph told his brothers the dream, however, it was very hard for them to take it in; they responded harshly toward Joseph because they thought that the youngest member of the family, and the father's favorite, was thinking about abusing that position in order to control them. As a result, Joseph's brothers rejected him.

The straw that broke the camel's back, however, was Joseph's second dream. He told them, "Listen to this dream I had: we were binding sheaves of grain out in the field when suddenly my sheaf rose and stood upright while your sheaves gathered around mine and bowed down to it." His brothers responded, "Do you intend to reign over us? Will you actually rule us?" And his brothers hated him even more because of his dream and what he had said (Genesis 37:5-8). They expressed such disgust to their father that he reprimanded Joseph not to have such dreams because they are dreams that are humanly impossible.

CONFRONT OPPOSITION

While God was showing Joseph the future blessing that was waiting for him, the enemy quickly mobilized his best soldiers to prevent Joseph by any possible means to keep

God's dreams from being fulfilled. The enemy must have planted thoughts in the minds of Joseph's brothers such as, "We cannot allow him to rule over us." That is why they threw Joseph into an empty well and abandoned him. After his own brothers sold him into slavery, they must have thought, "He who was going to rule over us is now just a simple slave. Who is going to bow down before a slave?"

CONFRONT DEPRESSION

You must understand clearly that the enemy's purpose for adversity is to discourage you so that you lose hope and bury your dreams. That well in which Joseph found himself symbolizes the darkness, depression and loneliness that a leader sometimes must face because of envy.

Joseph had to endure some very difficult moments that were caused by the people whom he loved the most, but he did not let adversity destroy his dream. After suffering the rejection of his family, he had to learn to depend completely on God. As a result, he developed a more intense prayer life, which helped him to fulfill God's purpose in adversity to strengthen his character and to conquer his dream.

If you overcome adversities and put your confidence in God, He will give you the victory and fulfill your dreams.

FACING OBSTACLES

Behind the visible world there is a whole, invisible realm. A simple veil is all that separates the two. In the visible world, Joseph faced temptation. He was slandered and thrown in jail. But in the invisible realm, in the midst of adversity, Joseph never stopped nurturing his dream. He was certain that God had already established in His agenda a time when his dream would be fulfilled. You must have the same attitude. Even though the circumstances may seem adverse, you cannot weaken. You have to remain strong in your faith until you have the victory.

In leadership, it is essential that you learn the basic spiritual principle of the parable of the talents (Matthew 15:14-30): «*Whoever is faithful in a little will also be faithful in much*». In Joseph's life of slavery, the only thing that he had was his integrity, but God tested even that. God does not trust you with His work until your character, and your integrity have been tested. You will face trials and difficulties, but the important thing is to fight until you overcome them. Remember that after Joseph was tested, the "little" that he had was blessed and became "much."

Consider some of the obstacles that Joseph had to face during his journey to blessing:

1. *Envy.* In Proverbs 27:4, Solomon says, *"Anger is cruel and fury overwhelming, but who can stand before jealousy?"* Jealousy is like a giant that rises up to destroy

your dreams. It is what led Joseph's brothers to plan his destruction and throw him into that well.

2. *He had to endure rejection.* Every vision given by God is going to meet opposition. This is generally seen in leaders who resist change. For them, it is not easy to accept innovations. If the people of Israel had not rejected Jesus, human history would have been very different, but God always uses adversity to bring a great blessing to His children. The transgression of the Jews was the salvation of the Gentiles. (Romans 11:11).

3. *Faith to endure changes.* After suffering the rejection of his own brothers, Joseph had to face so many changes that only the grace of God could sustain him. He had to leave his father, which was quite difficult for him, because they had a very close knit relationship. He found himself day and night like a slave in a foreign land, chained behind the gates. There were so many difficult changes that the only thing that kept him spiritually fed was his faith in the dream that God had given him. He knew that he had to wait with patience.

4. *He had to confront temptation.* "I find more bitter than death the woman who is a snare, whose heart is a trap and whose hands are chains. The man who pleases God will escape her, but the sinner she will ensnare" (Ecclesiastes 7:26). The spirit of seduction surrounded Joseph's life and tried to break him, but he remained

firm in his faith because he had made the decision not to fail God by giving into the deceptive desires of the flesh. That was how he succeeded in fleeing that situation. He preferred a physical prison to an emotional one. God protected him in the midst of his adversity; He honored him and opened his mind so that he could understand what happened in the spiritual world. It was easy for him to interpret dreams because he had endured tests. He had filled himself with the power of the Spirit while maintaining daily, close communion with God.

All of these tests produced a strong character of integrity within Joseph. When God gave Pharaoh a dream that no one could interpret, a man recommended Joseph for he had interpreted his dream. They sent him to get Joseph out of jail. At that point, the character that God had developed in Joseph revealed itself. The ruler saw that Joseph's spirit was superior to that of any other person, and he put him in charge of all the land of Egypt.

A DREAM MADE INTO REALITY

How many years did Joseph have to live through before God showed him his dream fulfilled? What did he think when he saw his brothers who had gone to Egypt in search of food, throwing themselves down before him reverently without recognizing his identity? He must have had a heart full of gratitude to God when he realized that no man can oppose the fulfillment of dreams given by God.

GOD STRENGTHENS US SO THAT WE CAN FULFILL OUR DREAMS

Two years after beginning the ministry, when my church was still very young, we invited one of our pastor friends to preach to us one Sunday. The Spirit flowed through him, bringing a prophetic word. The sermon that day was about the prophecy: God´s dream revealed to us. He spoke about what God was going to do in our church and how He was going to raise up leaders and establish the vision of cell groups. He communicated that the ministry would grow extensively. He even spoke that many people would not understand the vision and that they would criticize it but once we had passed through that time of testing, the faithful ones would be raised up in leadership like captains of their respective ministries. All of this happened in 1990, after that my wife decided to enter the political arena some people did not understand how important it was for Christians to take this step. It even caused some leaders to leave the church. Regardless of this exodus, many people were getting saved, and that is when we began to grow.

A greater unity came into the leadership; the ties of friendship and support became much stronger among the team members.

When we learn to endure difficulties together, to cry together in our trails and also to laugh together, love grows stronger, fellowship is more sincere, and the relationships are more transparent.

In the precious leadership that forms MCI, we incorporated those who have the strength to endure any stormy test. Those are the ones who are standing with us by our side today, shoulder to shoulder.

TEACH THE CHURCH TO PRAY

Two months before the assassination attempt, we had pushed ahead and began using one of the biggest auditoriums in Bogota: The domed stadium known as "El Campín." We had two meetings every Sunday, and God was blessing us in an incredible way. At that time several precious prophets of God visited us, and one of them prophesied saying, "Satan has thrown his dirtiest tricks at you, but I have decreed that no weapon formed against you will prosper and that death will not hurt you. I will put angels before you and all around you to guard you and your whole family, and I have established this decree in the heavens: The devil cannot return to touch my servant."

When we heard this prophetic word, we did not understand it. We did not know if it was referring to something in the past. We did not understand it until two months later, when the assassination attempt occurred.

That Sunday, I had preached on the power of blessing and acted out the prayer to the brothers. I told them, "We do not know how to pray because genuine prayer has more groans than words. We should let the Holy Spirit intercede for us with unspeakable groans" (Romans 8:26). Then I knelt down and I began to groan, helping them understand the way that God wanted us to pray.

THE POWER OF INTERCESSION

The assassination attempt took place after the second meeting. The news traveled quickly through the whole country. Some people said that they had killed me. Others said that I was disfigured, still others said that I was in the hospital. Immediately the church remembered my message of that day, and all the believers began to groan in the spirit day and night. All of the leaders were interceding, begging God to let me live. "God, don't take our pastor; Lord, give back his life; we need our pastor." My wife and my daughters could not stop praying. Claudia knew that my life depended on persistent prayer. The atmosphere was so confusing that even my brother-in-law, who is a doctor, told my sister-in-law after examining me, "Cesar can't be saved. It would take a miracle. If that happens, I will become a Christian." As you should imagine, my brother-in-law is today one of the doctors who helps us in the ministry.

A WOMAN OF FAITH

But the most amazing thing of all was the faith of my wife. She did not accept, even for a moment, the idea that I would die. She would not allow anyone with a negative attitude to approach her or to feel sorry for her. She only wanted to see people who were proven in their faith. She came to have such security that I was going to recover that, next to the bed where I was lying unconscious, she signed the promissory notes for our new home. She wanted to give me that surprise when I woke up. Due to her faith, the level of intercession grew - not only in our family - but in the whole church. Ten days later, God glorified Himself and practically raised me from the dead.

By enduring this test together, the whole team became much more strongly unified. Because I could not resume my leadership position in the church, my leaders told me, "Pastor, don't worry, we will handle everything as if you were right there in the church with us." The adversity that we endured created greater commitment, faithfulness and love among us. Now, I no longer need to be present in the church preaching because the team of pastors does it as well as if I was there doing it myself.

WE LONG TO HAVE THE DREAMS OF GOD

Joseph understood from the time that he was very young that God has to communicate with each one of His children to reveal the future to them. Joseph could endure all of the storms that rose up against him because of the visions and dreams that were revealed to him by God. He rested with complete assurance that whatever God revealed in the language of faith, would be fulfilled. While his physical condition was being tested daily, his spirit rested on those dreams that God had given him. Without becoming desperate or allowing doubts to enter his mind, he succeeded in maintaining firm faith, without wavering, so that one day he would fulfill all that God had promised him.

Each pastor and leader who can understand that God does not discriminate against anybody, and knows that He wants each one of His children to be able to fulfill their dreams, will grow much faster than they can ever imagine. The dream of Henry Ford was that each American would have a vehicle, and it happened. Now we should understand that the dream of God is that each one of His children will receive His dream and then fulfill it. The question that the Lord asked the prophet Isaiah was, "Who has believed our announcement, and around whom has the Lord placed His arm?"

DREAMS ARE THE LANGUAGE OF GOD

To some people, it's hard to believe that God speaks through visions and dreams, but didn't He speak to Mary that way? And, He told Joseph in dreams that he would flee

Egypt. Later, he told him again in another dream that he would return. He spoke to Peter in a vision so that he would visit the house of Cornelius. He manifested Himself to Paul after his conversion, in visions and dreams, and on one occasion He told him, again in a vision, to visit Macedonia. How did John receive the revelation of the Apocalypse? We can see that all of these men of God learned to speak the language of faith through visions and dreams, and in general He was pleased with each one of them.

The dream that we have as a church is not a new dream but rather the continuation of what Jesus began—which is known as the *Great Commission*—where we not only go out to win souls but also strengthen them until they can be true disciples of Christ who can also reproduce themselves in others. In this way, we see that the dream of God - of having the nations discipled, will be a great reality.

Dear reader, I invite you to add your faith to mine and together we can reach our cities and nations for Christ through the Government of the Twelve.

Chapter 4

TEACH THEM ABOUT THE POWER THAT LIES WITHIN THE WORD

"In the beginning was the Word, and the Word was with God, and the Word was God. He was with God in the beginning. Through him all things were made; without him nothing was made that has been made."

John 1:1-3

THE WORD OF POWER

Jesus is the Word of God that has always existed. John presents Him as the logos, a Greek word that was used to indicate intelligence, wisdom and expression. Through the use of this word, we see that the wisdom and intelligence of God were in Jesus since the beginning and that He is the author of everything that exists. In His infinite love, He decided to take human form in order to speak the truth of God in our own language.

Jesus is the living Word of God, the same Word that was with God during the creation of the world when He said,

"Let there be light." The Word of God moved into action in perfect harmony with the Holy Spirit, and they succeeded in transforming chaos into something useful and beautiful. Paul said, "This is the word of faith that we preach," the word that transforms circumstances.

It was necessary for the Word to become flesh. Imagine, all the authority of God, all of the divine power concentrated in only one person named Jesus of Nazareth. Each word that went out of His mouth was dynamite. When demon-possessed people were in one of His meetings, Jesus just said, "Be quiet and come out of him." And the demons left the bodies of those people. The people were shocked and said, "Who is this man who speaks with such power that even the demons obey?"

When Jesus decided to go with His disciples to another region, a great storm arose while they were in the boat. "A furious squall came up, and the waves broke over the boat, so that it was nearly swamped. Jesus was in the stern, sleeping on a cushion. The disciples awakened Him and said to Him, "Teacher, don't you care if we drown?" He got up, rebuked the wind and said to the waves, "Quiet! Be still!" Then the wind died down, becoming completely calm. He said to his disciples, "Why are you so afraid? Do you still have no faith?" They were terrified and asked each other, "Who is this? Even the wind and the waves obey Him!"

THE WORD WAS REVEALED TO THEM

Jesus wanted to test their understanding of what He had taught them. Did they really understand His true nature? The best way to know was by allowing a small test in their lives. Although Jesus was sleeping, they thought that everyone who was in the boat was going to die. As fishermen, they knew that in a similar situation only a miracle could save them. Something similar happens when we have to pass through tests as children of God. We can feel that the wind is blowing against us and that no matter how hard we try with our own efforts to move forward, it all seems in vain. That is when we decide to wake up the Master and ask Him, "Lord, don't you care that we are all going to die in this test?"

When Jesus put Himself at the forefront of the situation, rebuking the wind with only two words, the sea had to become calm in the face of the One who spoke. The disciples were perplexed by the word of authority that came out of Jesus' mouth. The question that came to their minds was, "Who is this?" They saw what Jesus had done; no other human being had ever done it. Their spiritual eyes were opened and the incarnate Word of God was revealed to them. They saw the proof that He who could take control over the forces of nature and make them obey Him, as a servant bows before his master, could not be any less than God Himself. This really helped the disciples' faith because now they had the assurance that this man was truly the Son of God.

NO ONE WAS LIKE HIM

On one occasion, the religious leaders were very jealous and wanted to catch Jesus, so they sent soldiers to accost Him. When the soldiers returned empty-handed, the religious leaders asked them, "Why have you not brought him?" They replied "No man has ever spoken like this man." Even the people who were living far from God could see that the message that Jesus spoke was nourishment and hope for the people. They could not compare what they were hearing with what the religious leaders were teaching. Those men remained amazed by the words of life that came out of the Master's mouth.

All of God's authority and power is conveyed in Jesus. John, one of those who had been close to Jesus, said, "We have seen his glory, the glory of the One and Only, who came from the Father, full of grace and truth" (John 1:14).

HE WANTS TO RELATE TO US

The Lord spoke prophetically through the writer of Proverbs: "I rejoice in this whole world and delight in mankind.... Blessed is the man who listens to me, watching daily at my doors, waiting at my doorway. For whoever finds me finds life and receives favor from the LORD. But whoever fails to find me harms himself; all who hate me love death" (Proverbs 8:31, 34-36).

The Lord made it very clear that He desires to relate to us in a delighted way and that everyone who makes the effort and perseveres in listening to His Word diligently will be the kind of person who will receive the Lord's endorsement in everything that he undertakes. Isaiah said that if we wanted to have wise tongues, He should awaken our ears every morning to hear like wise men (Isaiah 50: 4). The relationship must always be a two-way relationship; God speaks to us and we listen to Him. This relationship prepares us so that the Word of God can dwell in us.

THE POWER OF WORDS SPOKEN BY JESUS

The family of Lazarus was very distressed by all that had happened to him because four days had already passed since his death, by the time Jesus came to his tomb and demanded to roll back the stone. Martha, Lazarus' sister, was shocked because what Jesus was doing was very unusual. She told Jesus, "Lord, he stinks already because it has been four days." Jesus knew very well what He was doing; He was teaching a great lesson not only to this family but to us as well: When we have a good relationship with the Word of God, that Word will give life to those things that have died. His response was, "Have I not told you that if you would believe, you will see the glory of God?" Jesus did not enter into a long period of prayer, He simply thanked the Father for having listened. Later, He cried out in a loud voice, "Lazarus, come forth!" The Word of power had been expressed and immediately began to run its course to fulfill its purpose. It crossed the heavens and went even to the bosom of Abraham, where Lazarus was. The voice of Jesus rumbled through the whole place and perplexed millions of beings that lived in that site. Everyone turned to look at Lazarus, who understood that it was the voice of His Lord and Master, which he should immediately obey. Even though he was in the earth, he did not want to lose the privilege of staying at Jesus' side, the incarnate Word of God.

That was how he came back to life and came out of the tomb. When Lazarus opened his eyes, he was bound hand and foot with grave clothes. Jesus looked at him and told his disciples to untie him and let him go. Jesus had to be very specific with each of His words because each one activated legions of angels as it left His mouth, and they did whatever He said. Jesus said, "Truly, truly, I say unto you, the hour is coming and now is when the dead will hear the voice of the Son of God, and those who hear will live. Do not be amazed at this because the hour will come when everyone who is in a grave will hear His voice" (John 5:25, 28).

If Jesus had not been specific in mentioning Lazarus by name, that day could have been the day of the resurrection of the dead.

SAY THE WORD AND THE MIRACLE WILL HAPPEN

There was a man who surprised the Lord by the kind of faith he had. The man was a centurion whose servant lay in bed with a terrible sickness. However, the centurion did not ask for Jesus to be present in his house for the miracle to occur, he simply requested, "Send your word and my servant will be healed." Now, this man could make a suggestion like this because it was all based on the analogy that, "I am a man of authority, and I know how to obey orders, but I also have people under my authority who obey my orders. Jesus, whatever you say will happen because there is no other being in the universe that has more authority than you have. And whatever you say will happen exactly as you have said it." (Matthew 8:5-13)

The Lord took the faith of this man as an example and emphasized that no one in all of Israel could be found with the same kind of faith. This centurion saw Jesus as more than a person; he saw the eternal Word of God. Jesus is the Word of God dressed in a human body. If we believe in His Word, we are growing in Jesus. Everyone who is one of Jesus' sheep hears His voice and follows Him, and He gives them eternal life.

When we read the bible, we have the Word of God, but there is a moment when we feel that the message that we are reading is the specific Word of God for our lives, and this brings a great conviction into our hearts. Then we are sure that the miracle has already happened.

One of the most important aspects in the life of a believer is to believe the voice of God. Try to picture in your mind what happened: The centurion was a Roman army officer who was in charge of 100 soldiers. Although he was a respected man, with honors and awards, he had a compassionate heart and loved his servant who was sick and at the point of death. Each order that he gave to his subordinates was obeyed without question; they simply obeyed. But when he found himself facing sickness, even though he spoke to it, it would not submit to him. When he saw that the demons and the sicknesses submitted to whatever Jesus said, he understood that he would find his answer in Jesus.

ARGUMENTS THAT WILL BENEFIT YOU

The Jewish elders looked for Jesus so that they could say to Him, "It is righteous that you grant this to him because he loves our nation and has built a synagogue for us." Each argument that occurred before had become arguments that turned out to benefit him. These two arguments that favored the centurion continue to be just as powerful today: to love the nation of Israel and to build the kingdom of God.

Do you love the people of Israel? Do you pray for the peace of Jerusalem? This would be a good argument in your favor. It is written, "Blessed are those who bless you." God clings to each word that comes out of the mouths of

His people. Are you committed 100% to God and to His work? Are you making the effort to establish the kingdom of God in this season?

Consider the experience of one of the pastors who has worked at our side for years. One day, while he was driving his car, he felt like some strange hands took control of the steering wheel. That afternoon, he suffered a terrible accident. He felt as if his head had been separated from his body. That night, I was going to preach in the place where he was serving the Lord. Anguished because of the situation, his wife told me about his deteriorating health and her concern that he might end up paralyzed.

That day, I was sure that there were arguments in favor of that man because of all the seeds that he had planted for the work of the Lord. As I thought about it, the Spirit told me, "At two o'clock in the morning he will begin to get better." His wife went to the clinic and told him the news: "You're going to start getting better at two o'clock in the morning." That night, they both stared at the clock the whole time. When the hour came that had been indicated by the Spirit, he felt the touch of God in His body. His glorious presence flooded the room.

The following day, when I went to visit him and saw that the man's level of faith had risen, I laid my hands on him. At that moment, he sprang out from the bed and has remained completely cured by the power of Jesus Christ.

DARE TO SPEAK WITH FAITH

God gave each of us a measure of faith that becomes the key to conquering those things in the natural that would otherwise be impossible to conquer. Paul said, "According to the measure of faith that God has given to each one." Maybe you thought that you did not have faith, but God equipped you with a certain capacity to believe, and the only way to make faith grow inside your heart is through the relationship that you have with the Word of God. Perhaps the great men of faith were not even aware that they had great faith because their only concern was to please God in everything that they did.

When they found themselves in urgent situations, they simply exercised faith. When Joshua was conquering the Amorites, he found himself in a situation that impeded the successful completion of his goal. Daylight was disappearing, and nightfall would be a huge ally for his adversaries. But in a daring act of faith, Joshua spoke to God in the presence of Israel: "O sun, stand still over Gibeon, O moon, over the Valley of Aijalon." So the sun stood still, and the moon stopped, until the nation avenged itself on its enemies (Joshua 10:12-14). What gave Joshua so much courage to proclaim such a prayer? The same word that he had received from God: "No one will be able to stand before you all the days of your life; as I was with Moses, so I will be with you. I will not leave you or abandon you." That word given by

God was something that burned like a fire inside his heart, and he felt that the opportunities for conquest should be maximized. For that reason, he spoke in the presence of God so that His hand would move, causing the miracle. And he did not pray timidly or secretly; all of Israel heard him. His energetic voice was also heard in the heavens, and because of this man's prayer, the normal course of the day was altered. This came to be the longest day in history because the sun did not go down until Joshua's army had killed all of his adversaries.

THE MIRACLE SHOULD BE BORN IN US FIRST

When the Lord gave me the word, "Dream about a very big church because the church that you will pastor will be as numerous as the stars of the heavens and the grains of sand of the sea so that you will not be able to count the multitude," the multitudes were already burning in my heart, and I knew that the few sheep that I had would become uncountable multitudes. In that time, I shared my goal with a pastor friend: "I will have a church of 3,000 people." He quickly laughed and with a joking expression said, "Your faith is big." But a few years later, I had accomplished my goal, and I knew within me that I could not settle for that because what God had spoken to me had not yet been fulfilled. I had to go for a bigger challenge. When we got to 10,000 members, a pastor in the city told me, "Wouldn't it be good if you dedicated yourself to caring for those people that you have instead of thinking so much about winning more people?" My firm response was, "As long as there are 7,000,000 people in this city who do not know Jesus, how can I be satisfied with what I have accomplished? I will not rest until I see my city and my country rendered at the feet of Jesus."

THE POWER OF THE PROPHETIC WORD

God has a very special way of surprising His children. This is what happened with the prophet Ezekiel when the Lord led him to a wide valley full of dry bones, which were spread all over the countryside. The Lord asked Ezekiel, "Will these bones live?" The prophet responded, "Lord God, you know" (Ezekiel 37:3).

It is so good to know that our God never changes and that He has to confront us with our circumstances. He leads us to look at them face to face so that through faith and the word of authority we transform our circumstances. Our great challenge is to see our nations transformed by the power of Jesus, but the response is in our mouths. "Then he told me: Prophesy over these bones and tell them, 'dry bones, hear the word of God.'" (Ezekiel 37:4). Paul said, "How, then, can they call on the one they have not believed in? And how can they believe in the one of whom they have not heard? And how can they hear without someone

strategic
Preaching

preaching to them? And how can they preach unless they are sent?" (Romans 10:14-15).

The only thing that can bring life to any nation is the preaching of the Word of God, but it should be strategic preaching. I know that the best strategy is through cell groups where a personalized ministry can be developed and where each person that the Lord puts in our care can be ministered to as it is needed.

WE SHOULD PREPARE THE ATMOSPHERE FOR CONQUEST

A few years after having started the church, we got a great burden to pray, as a church, for the redemption of our nation. This led us to beg for God's favor with fasting and prayer. As a congregation, we fasted for three days, 7 times a year, for a period of about five years, until we felt that the heavens had opened and the blessing of God began to fall on our city and our nation. Unbelievers began to sympathize with the Christians, and we began to gain respect and credibility within the society. The percentage of Christians began to grow at an accelerated pace throughout the nation. Despite the social crisis that the nation was experiencing, the gospel continued to be spread rampantly.

Today, the gospel is preached in homes, in businesses, in universities and even in parks. The preaching of the gospel helped us to be able to raise up a whole army of men, women and youth that are as firm as valiant frontline warriors, proclaiming that Jesus is Lord, for the glory of God the Father.

RECLAIM YOUR LEGAL RIGHTS

The prophet Ezekiel received the legal right from God to reclaim the restoration of his people. When you believe and become full of faith, you can move in the supernatural realm. This will completely renew your mind, producing change that will even effect the way you see things:

- You will see them with the eyes of God instead of with your natural eyes.
- You will be able to have the vision given by the Spirit of God and not by your own imagination.
- You will speak the Word of God and not your own words.
- You will see with your own eyes all that God does.
- It will be easy for you to see one miracle after another.

God said, "Ask of me and I will give you the nations as an inheritance and the ends of the earth as your possession" (Psalm 2:8). Within the faith that God has given to each of His children, He stipulated the legal rights, which are the decrees established by Him to protect and bless His children. When we understand this, we will be transformed from being a failure into being successful. You will see the miracle of transformation in your community because all of the sterility will flee and great multitudes will come.

GOD WANTS TO TEACH US TO SPEAK PROPHETICALLY

Just like a loving father with his son, God was instructing the prophet so that he could act in a level of authority that he did not know before. He led him to prophesy in stages until he could see that those bones were transformed into a great army that stood up, firm and were ready for conquest. It is important to see that the prophet's obedience immediately stands out. He said, "So I prophesied as I was commanded, and as I was prophesying, there was a noise, a rattling sound, and the bones came together, bone to bone. I looked, and tendons and flesh appeared on them and skin covered them, but there was no breath in them" (Ezekiel 37:7 8).

Everything that the prophet was experiencing was in the spirit. God had taken the prophet's spirit and opened the spiritual world so that the state of his people would be revealed to him and so that the course of his nation's history could be changed through the prophetic word. The spiritual death would be absorbed by life, and the nation would experience a great revival.

Although this prophecy was directed primarily to the people of Israel, it is still a lesson for us today on how to serve God. As we enter into the world of faith and receive the visions of God, we can also see the faith being reborn in our people. When the prophetic word is confessed, it puts the Kingdom of God into action, and the angelic army begins to work based on what has been declared prophetically.

Chapter 5

TRAIN THEM IN
SPIRITUAL WARFARE

"For our struggle is not against flesh and blood, but against the rulers,
against the authorities, against the powers of this dark world and
against the spiritual forces of evil in the heavenly realms"

Ephesians 6:12

On that unforgettable morning of September 11, 2001, the world seemed to stop spinning as people everywhere were in shock as a result of seeing two of the historical monuments of New York collapse like a house of cards, that was caused by a demented terrorist attack.

Two thousand years ago, heaven was horrified to see the Son of God, Jesus Christ, being judged and condemned, resulting in the most horrendous death of that time—death on a Cross. But, the death of Jesus became the means of redemption for mankind. Adversity always has a purpose, the purpose of becoming a blessing. The blood of Jesus that was shed on the Cross of Calvary became the price paid by God to rescue mankind. It was the only way to save humanity from the slavery and oppression of the adversary. For this, I am certain that the blood of those thousands of people who died in the World Trade Center Towers on September 11th, 2001 was the price for the United States to turn its eyes to Jesus Christ so that the light of hope could be ignited. Undoubtedly, this ghastly occurrence has made people understand that not everything in life is buying and selling, getting married, separating and remarrying and living our lives only to satisfy the flesh. We must understand that inside of us there is a soul and it means nothing if a person takes care of his body, his beautiful home and expensive car if his soul is dry. The only thing that causes a soul to grow and prosper is the Word of God.

Jesus said, "My words are spirit and life" (John 6:63). Only the Word of God releases the spirit of life.

WHO IS OUR ENEMY?

Our enemy is a spiritual being created by God, who used to lead worship in heaven and used to enjoy his authority and a holy life. He was the first being that allowed pride to enter his heart, and in his arrogance he wanted to dethrone God so that he could have merciless control over everything. His greatest frustration was not being able to succeed in doing that and that is why he lost all of his privileges: He was quickly expelled from heaven upon which he became a secret enemy of the work of God. He was the first to arrive at the Garden of Eden where he successfully seduced the woman to disobey the divine command. Because of that, the Lord declared permanent war between Satan's seed and the woman's seed, warning them that she would crush his head and he would bruise her heel (Genesis 3:14-15).

His primary purpose is to remove God from the heart of man and block his mind so that the message of salvation will not be preached to humanity. Paul said, "And even if our gospel is veiled, it is veiled to those who are perishing. The god of this age has blinded the minds of unbelievers, so that they cannot see the light of the gospel of the glory of Christ, who is the image of God" (2 Corinthians 4:3-4).

This evil spirit, lurks in the streets, around corners, in many places, watching us. In this way, he finds many people who are unprepared because they do not want to take precautions. I am talking about a spirit whom the Lord called "prince of the powers of the air." This spirit is very well organized. It comprises a hierarchical rank, divided into principalities, powers, governors and hosts of evil. These spirits live watching each street, each city and each nation. When these spirits feel that revival is coming to a nation, they send the strongest territorial spirits to try to stop the spiritual awakening.

We should recognize that we are in open war against the powers of Hell. Evil can come to you through a bad friend, a bad woman, or from impure images that you accept in your mind. That is why the Bible gives warnings about friendships and strange women and the importance of taking care of your eyes, your hands and your feet. And, that is why we should learn to take control of our words.

We must be aware that we are in a battlefield. The enemy targets Christians because he has already captured the others.

HOW DOES HE ACT?

He established an empire of terror and is characterized by being:

1. Astute (Genesis 3:1).
2. Untruthful (Genesis 3:1-3).
3. Vengeful (Psalm 8:2).
4. Destructive (Isaiah 54:16).
5. Tempting (Matthew 4:7).
6. Accuser (Revelations 12:10).
7. He is the prince of demons (Matthew 12:24).
8. An assassin and the father of lies (John 8:44).
9. The prince of the powers of the air (Ephesians 2:2).
10. The dragon (Revelation 12:7-9).
11. A roaring lion (1 Peter 5:8).
12. He dresses like an angel of light (2 Corinthians 4:4).

HIS PURPOSE

The adversary's objective is for each child of God to leave the path of righteousness and to follow the path of sin. The Lord Jesus said, "Every kingdom divided against itself will be ruined, and every city or household divided against itself will not last" (Matthew 12:25).

Machiavelli said, "Divide and you will conquer." Satan's goal is to divide families, separate homes, and take control of people. James said, "What causes fights and quarrels among you? Don't they come from your desires that battle within you?" (James 4:1). Those passions that lead to hatred and carry people into war are fed by that hidden enemy who loves to see how one comes against others.

WHO WOULD FACE HIM?

The curtain will be pulled back from the minds of believers when we can understand the victory won by Jesus on the Cross of Calvary, where the enemy was defeated and stripped of all of his power and authority. All of humanity had been captured by Satan's deception and was suffering the effects of his unrelenting and unmerciful oppression. There was no way to remove the yoke from his neck because no human could stand before a being that was stronger and wiser. Each time that the enemy felt that someone could be raised up causing threat to his reign, he would rise up against him with all of his might.

When Moses was born, his throne shook, and he had all of the little boys killed. Something similar happened with Herod when he received the news that the King of the Jews had been born in Bethlehem. Satan believed that he was the owner of the whole earth and maintained a very powerful warning system because he did not want to let even one person live in freedom. The words that God spoke in the garden resounded over him: "From the woman will be born one who will crush his head and you will strike his heel" (Genesis 3:15).

When Jesus was baptized to initiate His ministry, the Spirit led Him into the desert to be tempted by the devil. After forty days of fasting, the tempter came to Him and attacked him using three of his most powerful weapons, but he began to be defeated in his own territory.

During the earthly ministry of Jesus, all the weapons employed by the adversary against Him had been used in vain until he decided to use his most powerful one—death. He seduced Judas' heart to betray Him and controlled the jealousy of the religious leaders so that with the endorsement of the people and the approval of the Romans they condemned Him to death and worst of all, death on the Cross. I believe that it never Crossed the enemy's mind that the death of Jesus would become the fulfillment of Biblical prophecies and in time would lead to his own destruction.

God, in His wisdom, had established that every curse that comes against the human race would be put on the body of Jesus to be destroyed on the Cross.

THE CROSS IS A DOORWAY TO RECONCILIATION

If you ask a Jew, what they think about the Cross, they would to tell you that it is a cursed place where the most dangerous delinquents of the nation die. When the first couple sinned, they were in the Garden of Eden. There were two trees in this garden, the Tree of Life and the Tree of the Knowledge of Good and Evil. If the man took the fruit of the tree of life, he would live forever; he would be like the angels who never die. But if he took the fruit from the Knowledge of Good and Evil, it would result in physical and spiritual death. The man chose the fruit of the forbidden tree. After he ate its fruit, God threw him out of paradise. They lost all of their privileges, but gained new sight into a very different reality than they had known before. Now they would know affliction, sickness, pain, poverty, ruin, loneliness, etc. They had to suffer the effects of their own sins.

Now God had to establish another tree. This tree was different. It had only two branches, one vertical, towards God and the other horizontal, towards the needs of the people. That tree was The Cross. By taking the fruit from the wrong tree, man remained outside of paradise, and God had to use another tree so that everyone who would eat of its fruit would have their relationship with God restored and would receive all of the benefits that man had lost through his sin.

WHAT DOES THE CROSS MEAN?

For Paul, the Cross was the place where the world had been crucified and him for the world (Galatians 6:14). Jesus never knew sin but He began to absorb the curses of all mankind at the Cross. Jesus became a kind of magnet that attracted the curses of people. Generational curses began to be attracted to the Cross. God gave such a clear understanding to the prophet Isaiah about the redemptive work, like to few prophets in ancient times. Isaiah wrote, "Who has believed our message and to whom has the arm of the LORD been revealed?" (Isaiah 53:1). And in the rest of the chapter he describes redemption, which was fulfilled some seven hundred years later.

Jesus took our place and suffered our punishment. Paul said, "Christ redeemed us from the curse of the law by becoming a curse for us, for it is written: 'Cursed is everyone who is hung on a tree'" (Galatians 3:13).

One of the men who died at Jesus' side believed in Him and told Him, "Lord, remember me when you are in your kingdom." Did Jesus tell him that salvation would come to him in a thousand years? No! He said, "today you will be with me in paradise." On the day that you give Him your whole life, that same day you will move from the curse to the paradise of blessing.

THE CROSS ANNULS THE ACT OF DECREES

Because of sin, arguments were established against us in the spiritual world. An argument is a legal right against us. How are arguments formed? These can come through curses that you inherited from your family or through words that your parents spoke against you in a moment of anger or in jest or by wanting to impose their authority, etc. They are also established by sins that we have committed, by words that we have said, and by thoughts that we have accepted.

I was teaching the leadership on this topic, and later we had a time of prayer to minister to them. When the atmosphere was full of the presence of God, my spiritual eyes opened and I had a vision of the Cross where Jesus was being crucified. Demons were moving around the Cross, holding arguments in form of decrees while the people were repenting and renouncing the curses that had come through their sins or through their pasts. Immediately, all of these arguments were taken from the demons' hands and nailed to the Cross. The demons were trying to take the arguments back, but while they were trying to do so, a fire came over all those decrees, and the demons disappeared.

While I was contemplating this vision, all the people that were in the auditorium were crying and many chains were broken off their lives. "And having disarmed the powers and authorities, he made a public spectacle of them, triumphing over them at the Cross" (Colossians 2:15).

"Where, O death, is your victory? Where, O death, is your sting? But thanks be to God! He gives us the victory through our Lord Jesus Christ" (1 Corinthians 15:55, 57).

BREAKING OPPRESSION

The day that Jesus died, the skies became dark covering the whole earth. That was the moment when the demons celebrated, thinking that, with the death of Jesus, they had gained entire control of humanity. The clouds of darkness represented the time of the demons departure from their confinements into gathering for a celebration. But they did not count on all that was to come against them. In the moment in which Jesus died, the Cross became a kind of magnet that would absorb all of the demonic powers as if they were little pins being carried on the magnetic current, toward the Cross. The death of Jesus on the Cross was already the way that the enemy was bruising the heel of the woman's seed because the heel is the weakest part of a man, and children are like the heel or the weak part of the woman. But as Jesus took His last breath, the heavens shook and the earth trembled. And all of the demonic powers were broken.

The Most High spoke:

"The earth trembled and quaked, and the foundations of the mountains shook; they trembled because he was angry. He shot his arrows and scattered the enemies, great bolts of lightning, and routed them" (Psalm 18:7, 14).

Psalm 149:5-6 says, "Let the saints rejoice in this honor and sing for joy on their beds. May the praise of God be in their mouths and a double-edged sword in their hands." The double-edged sword is the Word. In order to execute vengeance among the nations, punishment among the people, and to bind kings with fetters and nobles with chains, the Word must be applied. These kings are the demonic principalities of evil that Jesus vanquished, which were operating in the air, deceiving those who were gullible or unwary.

Consider the sayings of Agur:

"There are three things that are never satisfied, four that never say, 'Enough!': the grave, the barren womb, land, which is never satisfied with water, and fire, which never says, 'Enough!'" (Proverbs 30:16).

The Hebrew word for grave (sheol) refers to hell, which is never satisfied. The demons come from sheol, and they are never satisfied. Every uncontrollable desire in a human heart that produces slavery or complete dependence, is the work of a demon. If people are not freed from oppression, that desire will grow until it destroys them.

A LIFE OF INTEGRITY

Jesus completed His mission of bringing redemption to mankind, but it must be complemented by a complete surrender of our lives to Him. This will give us the right to become children of God and to participate in His divine nature, but our lives should be separated from the corruption of this world.

"Make a tree good and its fruit will be good, or make a tree bad and its fruit will be bad, for a tree is recognized by its fruit" (Matthew 12:33). In other words, the commitment to serve Jesus is a decision that each person must make. And if you have made that decision to serve God, then you should put it at the level of your commitment.

HELPING PEOPLE TO BE FREE

When we first began our ministry, helping people to become free of their burdens was what led us to spend long hours ministering to them day in and day out. Both my wife and I had received deliverance by that time, and we understood that there was no other way for the people to bear fruit except to go through deliverance. Extraordinary miracles began to happen by the power of God. People decided to commit themselves fully to the Lord, and the church began to experience life. They longed for the day to come when they could participate in the meetings.

Then soon, the good news of people being freed from demonic oppression began to reach people everywhere.

The need was so great in those lives that I gave myself completely to ministering deliverance. I dedicated days and entire weeks to minister to all kinds of people. Soon, I began to notice a tremendous physical exhaustion, and I told myself, "I should not be doing this work alone," so I began to raise up a team. Later, I allowed only one day per week to minister deliverance, but then the Lord made us see that in order to have better results the people should go to an encounter. That was how we began to minister to them in encounters, and God relieved the burden because we had an army of people supplying their needs from week to week.

If we succeed in helping each person understand that on the Cross of Calvary, the Lord Jesus completely defeated the demons. Also, He gave us authority to rebuke them in His name, we will see many lives transformed by the power of Jesus Christ.

Steps to ministering deliverance

1. *Bind the strong man (Matthew 12:29).* God gave you all authority to bind the adversary in the name of Jesus. That strong man, Satan, has to respect your word of authority because when you pronounce the name of Jesus He is present and will justify whatever you confess. When you bind the adversary, try to see in your mind that an angel

of God comes with a chain to bind him and rebukes him, removing him from the middle of the way and throwing him into the depths of the sea. Remember that what we bind on earth will remain bound in heaven.

2. *Resist Satan firmly (James 4:7).* God has prepared your life for war, and even though the adversary is a defeated enemy, he will try to resist you so that you think you do not have power. All that Jesus conquered was in the spiritual realm and people of faith are the ones who can understand and claim their rights. If you succeed in keeping yourself fully submitted to God, He will make it easy for you to resist the deceptions of the adversary, and he will flee from your life - your house, your finances and from your ministry.

3. *Be an expert in handling spiritual weapons (Ephesians 6:17).* Among the weapons that the Lord gives to his soldiers, there are weapons for defense and weapons to attack. A powerful weapon of attack is the confession of the Word. Remember that Jesus defeated the enemy, confessing the Word.

4. *Declare that the curse was broken at the Cross (Galatians 3:13).* The Cross is the total defeat against the demons, and when we stop preaching about the Cross, the curse begins to strengthen itself. All of the curses that came through the disobedience of the Word, as mentioned by Moses, (Deuteronomy 28:15) were conquered at the Cross.

5. *Confess the victory by His blood (Revelation 12:11).* The blood of Christ is a powerful wall of protection for us and our loved ones. The spirit of death did not dare to enter houses that were found protected by the blood of animals, when Israel was being set free, in their exodus from Egypt. If the blood of those animals had the power to protect them, how much more power does the blood of our Lord Jesus Christ have that can protect us today.

Chapter 6

HELP THEM WORK IN PARTNERSHIP WITH THE HOLY SPIRIT

"It seemed good to the Holy Spirit and to us..."

Acts 15:28

Upon receiving the revelation of divine glory, the prophet Isaiah saw the majesty of God and also the seraphims that covered their faces with one pair of wings and covered their feet with another pair of wings and flew with yet a third pair of wings. Upon seeing this, Isaiah was convicted of sin, confessed it, and heard the Lord saying, "Whom will I send? And who will go for us?" (Isaiah 6:8)

Those same words, given 700 years before Christ, are still echoing in this modern day. Whom will I send? To whom can I entrust the work of the ministry? God is spirit, and to do His work, He always looks for human help. God is looking for men who are willing to believe Him and to let Him guide them completely by His Spirit. Whom will I send? God is looking for honest and faithful people with steady homes who will not turn their backs on Him and will not be ashamed of their testimony. Whom will I send? And who will go for us? The prophet's response was, Here I am Lord, send me. Today, God is still waiting for a response. He is still looking for people who are ready to surrender their whole lives to the leading of the Spirit.

BEING GUIDED BY THE SPIRIT OF GOD

When the Lord said to Abraham, "Leave your country, your people and your father's household and go to the land I will show you" (Genesis 12:1), He gave him directions through which Abraham entered into a complete dependency on God, and he had to keep his faith at a high level in order to obey all that God had told him. We know that God wants to relate to each one of us, but how many of us have prepared ourselves to hear Him?

Since the day I was saved, I have been completely sure that God was calling me to the ministry. Since then, I have learned to hear the voice of God, which has guided me in each of the steps that I have taken. Although I did not know any Christian churches, He guided me to a church where I began my preparation to serve the Lord better. I continuously felt the burden for the lost, and this motivated me to bring the gospel to them.

Even though I was active in different areas of ministry for the first nine years, I spent most of my time pastoring small churches. Later, I understood that God was using that whole season as a training process so that I could fully enter the ministry that He had prepared in advance for me.

After God revealed to me His purpose for my life, He gave me the directives and I made the effort to act in accordance with His divine guidance. All of that was a renewal of my mind because when we are used to doing things our own way, we feel a certain security in what we do. Beyond that, when you must wait for God's order, you have the tendency to despair, because many times, His word does not come when you want it. Instead, you will find that you have no choice but to stand on the premise that God knows what the right time is and in order to be able to accomplish that, you must be patient.

WE SHOULD CONCENTRATE ON DEVELOPING THE VISION

During the first ten years of ministry, I was not interested in traveling because I wanted to birth that new child, (the church) in order to establish a solid ministry in it. That seemed, to me, to be the right thing to do before thinking about winning the nations for Christ.

In 1990, my wife and I went to Seoul, South Korea, for the first time in order to see Pastor Cho's church. We never imagined the impact that this trip would have in our lives. At that time, we had about three thousand members and about seventy cell groups. I was proud of the ministry, and was thinking that I had a big church. I was very satisfied. As I was attending one of Pastor Cho's meetings, I said to myself, "Lord, You brought me here to shame me; I feel humbled before you because I get the impression that I have not done much for your kingdom."

During that trip, something happened inside of us: many walls of structure were shattered and we began to believe God. If it had worked for Pastor Cho, it would work for us too. We returned from that trip having accepted the challenge to struggle for greater growth. We spent less than two minutes with Pastor Cho, but it was worth it, to see this man of faith who dared to believe God and set out to conquer; breaking away from all the traditional schemes of church growth. His ministry has been very innovative and has underscored the fundamental concept that the cell church is God's purpose for these end times.

HAVING A CLOSE RELATIONSHIP WITH THE HOLY SPIRIT

One of the most difficult challenges in ministry is to learn to have a close relationship with the Holy Spirit. For years, I have prayed to Him and cried out saying, "I want your direction; I long for your guidance, Lord." But to come to the place of such intimacy with Him is something that only happens when you fully surrender yourself, when you renounce your own interests and submit yourself to the divine will. When your dreams are united to His dreams, vision is what you receive from Him, and your goals become linked to God's goals. Then you can say that you are completely depending on Him; each step that you take, each thought that you accept into your mind and each word that you express with your lips, will give Him glory.

The Holy Spirit is the only one who knows the most intimate desires of God. He is the only bridge between the human and the divine, the eternal and the temporary. He is the only one who can help us bring the glory of God to this earth. Once Jesus ascended to heaven after His resurrection, the Holy Spirit was sent to take His place. Jesus could only leave the church in the hands of someone He could trust completely. The only person who met those requirements was the Holy Spirit. That is why the Lord said that when He came, it would be as a father for us: "I will not leave you as orphans" (John 14:18).

KNOWING THE HOLY SPIRIT

The Holy Spirit is very sensitive. That is why when Jesus was baptized, the heavens opened up and the Spirit of God descended on Him in the form of a dove. Doves are very sensitive; they are scared by the slightest noise.

Similarly, we can startle the Spirit with harsh attitudes and abrupt actions. To maintain intimacy with the Holy Spirit implies that you must guard that communion with Him daily, being careful not to let any attitude arise in your heart that will displease Him.

The Psalmist said, "Search me, O God...and see if there is any evil way in me" (Psalm 139:23-24). We should continuously tell God, "Search my life; maybe I am doing what seems right to me, but it is not right in your eyes. Holy Spirit, I want you to guide me in everything that I do." Many times, it is easier for us to become conformed to certain situations and to feel satisfied with what we have obtained, but when we maintain that intimacy with the Spirit of God, He does not allow us to monopolize the relationship or to get used to things as they are. But He Himself produces a motivation within us to follow Him with a spirit of conquest.

LEARNING TO DEPEND ON THE HOLY SPIRIT

I believe that one of the greatest privileges that I have had is that of being able to serve the Lord as a pastor. In more than ten years of serving Him in this area, we saw God's endorsement in a supernatural way. Everywhere we went, He filled the place. Every goal that we pursued was fulfilled. We enjoyed a certain amount of ministerial success, but within me arose great discomfort. I felt that what we had accomplished all those years, was still far below the demands of the spiritual needs of the people. That is why I dared to pray in an uncommon way. That day, I opened my heart to the Lord and said to Him, "Spirit of God, thanks for giving me the privilege of being part of your work, but I have made the decision to renounce the pastoral ministry. Spirit of God, I ask you that from this day forward you would be the pastor of the church and that you accept me as your co-laborer." I was praying from the depths of my soul.

Later, He approached me and said, "Why did you wait so long to tell me this? Until today, you were the pastor, and I was your co-laborer. When you got up to preach, you said, 'Holy Spirit, bless this message.' When you finished your teaching, you said, 'Lord, bless my words.' When you interceded for people, you told me, 'Holy Spirit, bless these people; move this way or that way.' You were acting as the pastor, and you had me as your co-laborer. Even in the meetings with your team of leaders, you taught them for hours and then said 'Holy Spirit, bless all that I have said.' But son, I am very glad that you have prayed this prayer and that you have given me your ministry. From now on, I am going to be the pastor, and you will be my co-laborer. You cannot even imagine what will happen in your ministry."

Since that day, the Spirit of God has taken the prayer I made very seriously, even to the point that He Himself indicates to us what days we should be in Colombia and when to travel to other countries.

He shows us when we have done our part and when He is in charge of the rest. He is the one who directs us to each area that He wants us to conquer.

BE TRUE TO THE VISION

As leaders, we have the responsibility to form the character of Christ in our disciples. The lessons of being an example will be greatly impressed in their hearts. The words that we speak and our attitudes will either motivate them or take away their motivation to keep moving forward. The direction that we give them in ministry and the goals that we establish will help them in a positive way and will affect the future of their ministry.

As I shared in my previous book, Successful Leadership Through the Government of Twelve, at the beginning of 1995, I began to prepare two hundred leaders to be sent out as pastors because we were planning to open two hundred churches in different parts of the city. I thought that this would be the fastest way to grow. Halfway through the year, my wife and I went to Seoul, South Korea to be part of a leadership conference that was attended by thousands of pastors. There, we had the opportunity to visit Pastor Cho's church, once again. While we were in the back part of the auditorium, I had a vision. My spiritual eyes were opened, and I saw Pastor Cho dressed like an athlete, running towards me with a torch in his hand. He ran to me and gave me the torch. As soon as I took the torch, the Holy

Spirit spoke to me and said, "Son, I am giving you the torch of multiplication. I gave you a vision of cell groups that is similar to the one that Pastor Cho has, but you wanted to introduce another vision within the vision, and this would take you out of my will. Son, I need you to dedicate yourself to the vision of cell groups." That day, I repented saying, "Lord, forgive me for trying to turn aside from what God had drawn up for me and for having worked according to my own criteria."

FOCUSING ANEW ON CELL GROUPS

When I returned to Bogotá, I met with the leaders that I was training. I shared the experience, and I asked them to forgive me for my previous ways of doing things, saying, "Let's go back again to the vision of cell groups." We set a goal of reaching five thousand cell groups over the next six months. It was a very difficult task. We did not reach the goal, but we went from 1,200 cell groups to 4,000 cell groups.

If we had not given the pastoral ministry to the Holy Spirit, my vision would have been completely limited, and we would not have conquered our dreams. But when the Spirit of God takes control of the church, He takes the responsibility very seriously. The apostles understood that when they said, "It seemed good to the Holy Spirit and to us..." (Acts 15:28).

In the ministry, we take great care to make sure that each decision that we make has the approval of the Spirit of God so that we never move outside of His purpose.

HOW TO BUILD A TEAM WITH THE HOLY SPIRIT

It is important to understand that in the work of God there are only two options, to do it in your own strength or to do it in His power. God wants you to work in complete intimacy with Him, to have Him be the main partner in you work. This decision that God wants for us to make can only be made from our own free will.

If you are inclined to do that, there are several things you should take into account:

He is a person

You cannot treat the Holy Spirit like He is something unreal or an object or an illogical being. The Spirit of God is a person as real as anyone you know and does not want you to ignore Him. He needs to hear your words. He likes it when you consult with Him. He likes it when you put each of your choices in His hands and allow Him to approve them.

That is why the early church was so successful. It developed fully and impacted the nations, although its early success came at a great cost.

Make Him your partner

It is important to understand that the Spirit of God wants to control your agenda completely. He wants to have the freedom to bring to fruition the changes that are required in your life. Remember, you are not building your own kingdom, you are helping to build His Kingdom.

To be partners with the Spirit of God implies that you will live a life of faith exclusively.

Depend on His resources

All the resources of God are administered by the Holy Spirit. He has everything that you need for His ministry, therefore, your relationship with Him should be excellent. To do the work of God is something supernatural, and makes our human impossibilities possible and our logic submitted to His council.

Before Jesus came into this world, people had known the ministry of God the Father. When the Lord Jesus was on the earth, the world was impacted by His redemptive work.

After Jesus ascended into heaven, the Holy Spirit became the only one representing both the Father and the Son. Therefore, He is the only one who determines what resources His servants need.

That is why our relationship with Him should be one of excellence.

Make Him the coach of the ministerial team

Human beings can make mistakes in choosing the proper team members. But the Spirit of God never makes such mistakes. He reveals to you the people with whom you should work. with, invest time with and who should be fomed into a leader. He will show you how to do all of it! One of the most difficult jobs of any leader is to form his team for the future. Choosing these people is as important as choosing who you will marry.

RENEW YOUR MIND

It is important to be very sensitive to the direction of the Holy Spirit and to always be ready to follow where He leads you. There is no question that your mind must be renewed every day to run the course that He has drawn up for you. The only way to renew your mind is to learn to spend time in His presence each day, drinking of His spirit. Through intimacy with Him, He pulls back the curtain and reveals to you what is in His heart for you to do.

TOTAL SURRENDER

The Holy Spirit wants to have intimacy with those who give over their lives totally to Him, not with those who try to tell Him how He should do things or what things He should do. He always wants you to submit to His guidance. This implies complete dependence on Him in everything that you do. In order for that to happen, every vestige of your ego must die.

COMMUNION

Plan each step that you take toward intimacy with Him. If you let Him direct your life, you will not make a mistake in anything because for Him the future is as clear as the present. And even though there are many things that you may not understand, if you do them in obedience to Him you will see positive results from your decisions. You should never do anything on your own; always give the Holy Spirit the time and the freedom to act. Sometimes, He says yes and sometimes no, but regardless of the direction that He gives to your life, you should be certain that He has everything under control.

RECOGNITION

May everything that we do bring God glory. It is not His desire for us to plan or seek our own glory. On the contrary, everything that we do should be exclusively for His glory. Many people as though they are owners of the gifts which belong to the Spirit of God. All of the gifts will end, and the only thing that will last is your character. Giving Him your life is to allow Him to shape your character and bring glory to His name.

Chapter 7

MOTIVATE THEM TO BE PEOPLE OF PRAYER

"We do have such a high priest, who sat down at the right hand of the throne of the Majesty in heaven, and who serves in the sanctuary, the true tabernacle set up by the Lord, not by man.... They serve at a sanctuary that is a copy and shadow of what is in heaven. This is why Moses was warned when he was about to build the tabernacle, 'See to it that you make everything according to the pattern shown you on the mountain.'"

Hebrews 8:1-2, 5

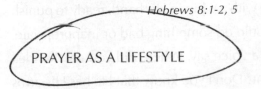

PRAYER AS A LIFESTYLE

In many families, the father is the figure of authority and the provider. The other members of the family make their needs known and expect the father to take care of them. In a similar way, prayer helps each believer communicate with the heavenly Father as the authority. We see Him as the provider that is why we believe that we should pray to Him when we need something. Your prayer life is the way you relate to God.

A successful prayer life, cultivates a close friendship with God. The question is how to come to the Father. How are you going to draw near to Him?

RELATING TO GOD AS YOUR FATHER

Thanks be to God for Jesus Christ; He is the only one that can make us relate to our heavenly Father. "Whoever has the Son has life, and whoever does not have the Son does not have life" (1 John 5:12). You must have the Son of God in your heart to have a strong prayer life.

One night at the beginning of my Christian life, I was praying in my room. Everything was completely dark, and I turned to God trembling with fear because I thought the Father was a very drastic person. I imagined Him to be seated on a throne with a whip in His hand, ready to punish me whenever I would do something bad or inappropriate. Suddenly, I heard a voice say, Where did you get the idea that God is like that? Don't you know that He has His arms extended, waiting for you to embrace Him? Immediately, in an act of faith, I threw myself into the arms of my heavenly Father. Since that moment, I have always felt very secure in my life. All of the emptiness caused by the lack of love from my earthly father was filled completely by the love of my heavenly Father.

Your prayer life is very important and requires you to find a quiet place to be alone with God each day without interruption. Sometimes I just want to have a short prayer time in order to appease my conscience, but I have realized that I cannot do that because as soon as I enter into the presence of God, all of my worries and anxieties disappear. The only thing I can do is surrender my life before Him.

The Lord has revealed, through His Word, various steps to take in order to establish an effective prayer life for relating to Him through the model of the tabernacle.

UNDERSTANDING THE TABERNACLE'S DESIGN

Every element of the tabernacle is very helpful in our relationship with Christ. The tabernacle was the sacred enclosure (sixty posts covered by a tent) that God established in the desert so that the people of Israel could come to Him. Moses spent forty days on Mount Sinai, where God gave him the design for the tabernacle and the tablets with the law etched upon them. God told Moses, "See to it that you make everything according to the pattern shown to you on the mountain." This structure became the house of God, the place where God had fellowship with His people.

The tabernacle of God has three parts:

1. The outer court: In the outer court, there were two key elements: the altar of sacrifice and the bronze platform.

2. The Holy Place: In order to get into the holy place, you had to cross through a gate with five curtains. The furniture of the Holy Place consisted of a bronze candle labrum, the table of the breads of the covenant, and the altar of incense. A curtain separated the Holy Place from the Holy of Holies.

3. The Holy of Holies: The heart of the presence of God was found in this last place which was the Ark of the Covenant with two Cherubims over it. Inside of it, there were the tablets of the law, a portion of manna, and the staff of Aaron, which had budded (*Hebrews 9:2-4*).

promise   *provision*   *protection*

ENTERING THE TABERNACLE

In order to enter the tabernacle, you have to pass through a gate. Only the people of God could do this.

Jesus alluded to this process in John, Chapter 10. *"I am the gate for the sheep"* He said (verse 7). *"Whoever enters by me will find pasture"* (verse 9). *"My sheep listen to my voice"* (verse 27), *"and they know me"* (verse 14). *"I give them eternal life"* (verse 28).

Only the true sheep of Jesus—those who have accepted Him in their hearts as Lord and Savior and are living for Him—will be able to enter the tabernacle.

Prayer:

«Lord Jesus, I completely give myself to you. I believe in you. I believe that you are the true God and through you I can come before the Heavenly Father. Thank you for letting me be part of the family of God and letting me enjoy all of the blessings that are represented in each one of the elements that forms the Tabernacle».

THE ALTAR OF SACRIFICE

The first thing that you see upon entering the tabernacle is the altar of sacrifice. That is where the priests used to offer animal sacrifices to God. This altar was a prototype of Christ because He became a pleasing offering before God. The whole purpose of the sacrifice of Jesus was to break every curse in your life. When you come to the altar, you can visualize the spotless Lamb of God, Jesus on the Cross of Calvary. There, you can imagine yourself crucified with Jesus.

Prayer:

«Lord Jesus, today I accept your death on the Cross as my death to sin. Today, I bring my whole human nature and crucify my passions and desires together with you. I thank you for all the blessings that I can receive through the Cross».

THE POWER OF THE CROSS

Moses raised the bronzed serpent in the desert so that those who had been bitten by serpents would be healed just by looking at it. In the same way, if we fix our gaze on the face of Jesus, the poison of sin that has entered into our lives will lose its effect and healing will come to our hearts.

Many people have tried to accept redemption by means of logic, but they continue to digress from the Lord's purpose and follow their own ideas because the only way to relate to God is through faith. Although it was established in the law that crucifixion was synonymous with a curse, Jesus accepted this fate through love for us so that we could become a blessing in Him.

Jesus transformed blessing from the curse now we can approach Jesus and find that, the fruits of blessing for each of us comes from the tree of the cross. We just have to reach out our hands and claim every rich blessing that Jesus won for us on the Cross, understanding that eating from His fruit, restores our relationship with God.

The blessing of salvation

The apostle Paul understood and affirmed this concept of salvation very clearly: *"I have been crucified with Christ, and I no longer live but Christ lives in me. The life I live in the body, I live by faith in the Son of God, who loved me and gave Himself for me."* (Galatians 2:20).

For Paul, Christ's death was not just Christ's death but Paul's, too! Later, he added, *"Those who belong to Christ have crucified the sinful nature with its passions and desires"* (*Galatians 5:24*).

Prayer:

«*Lord Jesus, today I come before you and I place all that I am, and all that I represent on the Cross of Calvary. In this moment, I crucify all of my passions, my desires, thoughts, and words with you. I recognize that I was lost, but your grace reached me. Now I am saved. I know that I am no longer condemned. I know that I am no longer going to hell. I know that I will not go back to the world because your salvation has reached me. Thank you, Lord, for rescuing me. I am thankful for what you have conquered for me. Thank you for the blood that you shed on that Cross. I know that right now it touches my life and cleanses me completely from my past. I know that I have received forgiveness for everything that has offended you because you have made me as white as snow. No iniquity will be able to rule over me ever again because your blood covers and protects me*».

The blessing of healing

The prophet Isaiah said, *"Surely he took up our infirmities and carried our sorrows...and by your wounds, we are healed"* (*Isaiah 53:4-5*). For some, it is easy to believe that salvation comes through the Cross, but it is difficult for them to believe that they will also receive healing.

Jesus conquered one as well as the other, it is a question of appropriating these benefits for ourselves by means of faith. In order to be able to bring clarity to this teaching, allow me to share the case of a woman who was an invalid who attended one of our meetings. I went up to her and I said, "Do you believe that Jesus can heal?" She responded to me firmly, "Yes." I gave her a brief orientation for about two minutes, and then I instructed her to keep her eyes fixed on Jesus throughout the whole service for when I was ready to pray for the sick, she would get up and walk. That lady left that meeting walking normally. Later, I asked her, "How did it go?" She replied, "I could see Jesus on the Cross. I could walk to where He was. I gave Him my paralysis, and I felt like it no longer belonged to me but to Him. And when you told me to get up and walk, I felt like my whole body was filled with great energy, and I had the strength to stand up and walk because I knew that the paralysis was not mine but His.

I know that healing comes as a result of our faith because everything is possible to him who believes.

Prayer: *Healing*

«Thank you Lord for conquering the miracle of healing for me 2,000 years ago. I know that those 39 lashes that you received on your back are medicine for my body. I believe in you, and I accept your healing for myself and for my loved ones. (You can name them specifically.)

Lord, I accept your healing in my marriage. I accept your healing for my parents, for my children, and for my relatives. Lord, by your stripes, we are all healed. I accept that miracle right now, and I resist every sickness and every pain in the name of Jesus. Thank you, Lord, for your healing. My blessing came from your broken body».

The blessing of prosperity   *Prosperity*

When Adam sinned, God told him that the land would be cursed because of him and would produce thistles and thorns (*Genesis 3:17-18*). When Jesus wore the crown of thorns on His head on the way to the Cross, however, He broke the curse that was in our lives and on our land.

Jesus became poor so that with His poverty we could become rich. Prosperity is not reserved for unbelievers; in fact, God already obtained it for His children. The apostle Paul said: "My God will meet all your needs according to his riches in glory by Christ Jesus" Paul also pointed to Jesus as God's instrument of bringing prosperity: "*For God was pleased to have all his fullness dwell in him, and through him to reconcile to himself all things, whether things on earth or things in heaven, by making peace through his blood, shed on the cross". (Colossians 1:19:20).*

Jesus represents all of the fullness of the Father, and one of His accomplishments on the Cross of Calvary was to get back the prosperity that man had lost because of sin. Jesus is God's treasure.

It really got my attention when I heard Dr. Cho say, "God put all his riches together in a person called Christ." When he said that, it was like a light came on in my mind and I saw the other side of the coin. We had always heard about the poverty of Jesus, but we rarely hear much about the truth that all the riches of the Father are concentrated in Jesus.

Prosperity is in God.

He gave it to Jesus, and Jesus gives it to His children. God reserved prosperity for you. This is something that is conceived inside of you through faith. Do not accept the spirit of poverty. Christ conquered it so that you could live in prosperity. God's desire is that you understand that the same word of God gives you the strategy to become prosperous so that His riches come into your life.

Tell the Lord in prayer that you want him to prosper you abundantly. Grasp in your mind that the veil of poverty, misery and inability, will be removed.

Prayer:

«Thank you, Lord, for taking my misery and my curse upon your head. Thank you, Jesus, because you took my curse, even the one that I inherited from my parents. I am free of every form of financial oppression. Thank you, Lord, because now I live under blessing. Thank you, Lord, that I now understand that it is not by human effort or what my energy can do but rather is your blessing in my life that brings

Body
mind
spirit

prosperity. I receive the mind of Christ, and from today on I will think in terms of abundance and prosperity. Lord, make my body, my mind, and my spirit the place where you bring your riches. God, give me your dreams; give me your creative ideas; give me your anointing so that prosperity can come to my life, to my family and to my ministry».

The blessing of multiplication

Just as death entered by sin, life entered by the redemption of the Cross. This life must be reproduced in the souls that you touch for the Lord. All those who look at the Cross of Calvary and assure that their disciples do it, they too, will be able to conceive the spiritual multiplication of souls within the community. Cell groups are nourished and multiplied at the Cross.

In one of the most critical moments in the life of Jacob, God gave him a great revelation (*Genesis 30:37-43*). Jacob carried the sheep to the drinking trough and put them down facing green branches of poplar, hazel and chestnut from which he had stripped the bark to show white streaks. When the animals saw these branches, they conceived the kind of offspring that Jacob wanted. That was how Jacob appropriated the miracle of multiplication.

The prophet Elisha told the widow to gather all of the jars she could borrow. The widow went racing through the neighborhood asking her neighbors for jars until she had all of the jars in the whole neighborhood. Later, they all ended up filled with the oil that came out of what little the widow had, and the sale of that oil was how the widow obtained provision (*2 Kings 4:1-7*). In the blessing of multiplication, every place in which a cell group is opened, will be filled by God because growth comes from God.

Prayer:

«God, I ask you to give me the anointing of multiplication. I ask that you revive everything I touch and give it life. Give life to my disciples, to my cell groups, to my community. Let everything that is dead be touched by your spirit of life. Lord, revive each person under my leadership so his or her faith will grow. Cause hope to grow in them and compensate them generously for what they have done for You. Today I see the multitudes that come to my ministry, and I declare that every form of spiritual sterility in my life is gone. From today on, I am a father to multitudes, in the name of Jesus».

THE BRONZE BASIN

After the sacrifice, the priest had to walk to where the bronze wash basin was and wash himself with the water that was in it. The water represents the Word of God, which should dwell in you abundantly. Commit to wash yourself with the water of God's Word daily. Jesus declared, *"Now you are clean by the word I have spoken to you"* (*John 15:3*) and *"He who is clean inside needs only to wash his feet"* (*John 13:10*).

Although the blood of the lamb cleans you, you need daily contact with the Word of God in order to maintain spiritual purity.

Prayer:

«Lord, today I wash myself with the water of your Word. Your Word is life. I need Your Word in my heart. Today, I want to commit to be faithful to You and to live my life being full of your Word».

THE FIVE POSTS

In order to enter the Holy Place, you have to pass the five posts which represent the five categories of ministries consisting of apostles, prophets, pastors, evangelists, and teachers, which are very related to the vision. The evangelist is the one who wins souls; the pastor is the one who shepherds them, the teacher is the one who disciples them; the prophet is the one who motivates them; and the apostle is the one who solidifies the ministry. Note in this vision the same person fullfils the five ministriesin different times.

Prayer:

«From this moment I accept your anointing for ministry over my life. Use me in whatever ministry you have for me. Make me sensitive enough to know how you want to use me. I always want to be faithful

to whatever you entrust to me because it is a privilege for me to have the character of Christ revealed in my life through any of your ministries. I know that by these ministries, thousands of people will be reached, edified, fed and ministered to».

THE TABLE OF THE BREAD OF THE COVENANT

Over the acacia table that was covered with gold there were the twelve breads of the covenant. *"Then you shall take fine flour and bake twelve cakes with it; two-tenths of an ephah shall be in each cake. You shall set them in two rows, six in a row, on the pure gold table before the Lord"* *(Leviticus 24:5- 6)*. This image gives insight into the groups of twelve, six cakes in each row. One of the rows represents looking at God. The other row represents looking at the needs of the people. You should want each of the members of your cell group to have a strong relationship with God and also to be concerned with the needs of the people who attend the cell group. Jesus said, *"I am the bread of life"* *(John 6:48)*. He is the One who gives you abundant life and reproduces it in your disciples.

Prayer:

«Lord, bless my ministry; bless the twelve disciples that you have given me and anoint them in their cell groups, in their lives, and in all of their commitments. You know each one of their needs, whether or

not they have been shared, and I ask today that your powerful hand
would be over them doing miracles and wonders. Thank you that your
power is working in them now'.

THE CANDLE LABRUM WITH SEVEN ARMS

This piece represents the abundance of the Holy Spirit. In the revelation that God gave to John, he saw Jesus as a spotless lamb with seven horns and seven eyes, which represent the seven spirits of God sent to the whole earth (*Revelation 5:6*). Consider the words of the prophet Isaiah, *"The spirit of the Lord will rest on Him, the spirit of wisdom and understanding, the spirit of counsel and strength, the spirit of knowledge and the fear of the Lord" (Isaiah 11:2)*. This represents the seven spirits of God: the spirit of Jehovah; Wisdom works together with understanding; counsel works together with strength; and knowledge works together with the fear of the Lord. You should make the decision to walk daily in a close relationship with the spirit of God, understanding that the fullness of the seven spirits of God rested upon Jesus (Revelations 5:6).

Prayer:

«Lord I ask you for the abundance of your spirit in my life. Give me
the spirit of wisdom and understanding, the spirit of counsel and
strength. I ask you to give me the spirit of knowledge and of the fear

of the Lord because I want to be a wise leader, full of abundant life.
Just as those spirits worked in the life of Jesus in His ministry, I ask that
from today on, they would be with me».

THE ALTAR OF INCENSE

We know that Jesus is the High Priest who intercedes for us before the Father. He went up to heaven and intercedes for each of us there. The altar of incense is a place of receiving mercy. Even if there are people who do not deserve forgiveness, you can extend mercy to each of them through intercession. Remember that mercy always triumphs over justice. When you enter into intercessory prayer, you can feel the same burden that is on the heart of God towards a world that is perishing.

Prayer:

«Dear God, just as you extended your infinite mercy to my life, today I
extend mercy over the lives of those who have hurt me. I also pray for
those who have never found your mercy and that you would make me
an instrument to touch their lives».

THE HOLY OF HOLIES

When Jesus died, the veil of the temple that separated the Holy Place from the Holy of Holies was pulled back. That is to say that through His body He opened a new path.

Before the death of Jesus, the only one who could enter the holy of holies was the high priest, and he could only enter one time each year. The priest came in with the blood of the sacrifice and first prayed for his own sins, then for the sins of all the people. God saw the blood and accepted the priest, and then he also accepted the sacrifice that he brought on behalf of the people.

Prayer:

«Thank you, Jesus, for taking your love to the Cross and pulling back the curtain that separated me from the Father. Today I have free access to your presence. I draw near to the throne of grace with confidence because I will find mercy there».

THE ARK OF THE COVENANT

The ark of the Covenant was inside the holy of holies, it represents the presence of God. The ark was the holiest thing to the people of Israel because it was the equivalent of having direct contact with God. All of the Jews knew that His presence was there.

When the Philistines took the ark, they suffered so many divine judgments over their lives and their territory that they decided to return it. They put it on oxen and carefully sent it back to the people of Israel.

THE BROKENNESS OF UZZAH

A long time later, when David took the ark to Jerusalem, he also carried it on oxen. At one point during the journey the animals got stuck in a piece of muddy land because it had been raining. Then the ark began to lean, and looked as if it were going to fall. Despite knowing that no one can touch the ark, a Levite named Uzzah from the children of Coat, reached out a hand to keep the ark from falling. In that moment, the judgment of God fell, and Uzzah died. (2 Samuel 6:6,7).

God was showing the people of Israel that mud is cleaner than the hand of man, that touching the ark with your hand is to mix the holy and the human. That was what brought the judgment of God in such a decisive way in the life of Uzzah.

THE BLESSING CAME OVER OBED-EDOM

David became so saddened because of what God had done to Uzzah that he said, "I will not carry the ark of God to Jerusalem." Then Obed-edom offered to keep the ark of God in his house. The whole time that the ark was there God blessed him and prospered his home and his family. This story illustrates that when you obey biblical principles, you and your family and your household will be blessed. Judgment only comes after some kind of profane act. Always remember that the presence of God is in the Ark of the Covenant. That is why any time that David wanted to consult over any matter, he would send someone to bring the ark to him. And God always responded.

A NEW COVENANT

God has always guided his people by His Word. The struggle that the Lord always had with Israel was because of how quickly the people forgot His Word; they also forgot Him and quickly fell into pagan rituals. The Lord said through the prophet Jeremiah:

"But this is the covenant which I will make with the house of Israel after those days," declares the LORD, *"I will put My law within them and on their heart I will write it; and I will be their God, and they shall be My people. They will not teach again, each man his neighbor and each man his brother, saying, 'Know the LORD,' for they will all know Me, from the least of them to the greatest of them,"* declares the LORD, *"for I will forgive their iniquity, and their sin I will remember no more" (Jeremiah 31:33-34).*

And, that is why Jesus affirmed, *"If you continue in my word, then you are truly disciples of mine; and you will know the truth, and the truth will make you free" (John 8:31-32).*

Prayer:

«Lord Jesus, I ask you to open my mind so that I can understand the truth of Your Word. Give me revelation and wisdom so that I always

know your will. Write Your Word in my heart with Your own fingers
so that it will guide me, protect me, and defend me against every
adversity. Thank you, Lord, for making me wiser than many of those
who have taught me. Your Word is a lamp unto my feet and a light
unto my path (Psalm 119:105)».

AARON'S ROD BUDS (NUMBERS 17:1-10)

In the day of Moses, a strong murmuring rose up against Aaron. In order to put an end to the conflict, Moses asked that one prince from each tribe take a dry staff and bring it before the presence of God, who would show the difference and would cause the staff of His choosing to blossom. This was how God confirmed the call of Aaron as priest.

That rod symbolizes the miracle of the resurrection. If we dare to believe God, the Lord will breathe the spirit of life over our ministries and over our family relationships and also over our finances. Even though hope may have dried up, these things can bud again with new life through prayer.

Prayer:

«Lord Jesus, I ask you to cause my ministry to bud again. Holy Spirit,
breathe over me so that I understand your purpose for my life. Lord,
bring new life to my finances. I ask you to breathe over me by your
Spirit and do a financial miracle now; just as you brought new life

to Aaron's rod, bring new life to my finances. And restore my family
relationships, in the name of Jesus».

THE PORTION OF BREAD

Manna, the food that God gave to the people of Israel when they were in the desert, represents the spiritual food for the people of God. Each believer should ask the Lord daily to provide a spoken Word for the day. "He wakens me morning by morning, wakens my ear to listen like one being taught" (Isaiah 50:4b). _ISAIAH 50:4_

Prayer:

«Lord, today I humbly bow in your presence, before You, where you dwell between Seraphims and Cherubims, and ask You to never let your Word be absent from my heart. I also ask that you help me to understand it clearly. Lord, let the manna of the spoken Word fill my heart so that when I read your word I can discern what you want me to say. Lord, revive my hopes, my finances, and my ministry in the name of Your Son Jesus Christ».

Chapter 8

CREATING LEADERS WHO ARE SURE OF THEMSELVES

"Fear of man will prove to be a snare,
but whoever trusts in the LORD is kept safe."
Proverbs 29:25

A CORRECT SELF-IMAGE

"Michael, you are a man of God," were the words spoken by a young girl who shared the scriptures to this man, but his response was, "No. I am a drug addict, and whoever is an addict will not be empowered to be a man of God." His words were the result of his conviction. "How can I be a man of God if my life is dominated by vices and I live in the streets as a result of them? I don't have friends, and all of my acquaintances have turned their backs on me. Not even death accepts me because every time I tried to take my life, I failed.

THE CROSS OF JESUS

While Michael looked at his past, he did not agree with the words that he had presently heard. He kept thinking that a man of God s something very sacred for him to be compared to. Although he did not understand a lot of things, he decided to give his heart to Jesus Christ. Nonetheless, these words continued to resound in his mind for several days. It was very difficult for him to accept that someone who had the kind of life that he had lived could change in such a short time. He remembered when, for a period of seven months, he had fallen into a profound depression and was completely isolated from normal surroundings. He had even reached the point that he neither desired to bathe himself, nor change his clothes. The only thing he wanted was to die, but death did not come.

After all that he had experienced in his life, he was asking himself, how he could be a man of God.

When Michael went to the encounter, the first thing he heard was that there was someone who understood and accepted him just as he was; His present condition did not matter. As he sat there listening, this statement caused him to recall a time when the effects of the drugs had worn off. But his state of mind was still in such depression that he actually went out onto a traffic filled street and threw himself down in hopes that a car would run him over, but Instead, they all missed him! In his despair, he decided to throw himself again, directly in front of a car, but instead, a gust of wind, pushed him so far away that he fell into a big hole. This hole was actually a landfill of trash from the entire city that had been dumped there! He did not fall all the way to the bottom but rather landed on a rock that supported him. He spent the whole night there until the following day. At that time, he was able to climb the mountain of trash and leave that site.

With all of the failures that this man had experienced, seeing that nothing was going well for him, he wondered how anyone could ever love him. He felt that no one could have any affection for him. All of this questioning was clarified in the encounter when he heard the teaching about the Cross. He could understand the great miracle of redemption - that God made a great exchange at the Cross of Calvary - where He took all of his sins upon His body. He learned that all of those who believe in Him can receive all the blessings that Jesus has prepared for us. This revelation awakened his faith in such a way that he did not want to spend any more time without obtaining his benefits.

THEY WERE RESTORED

Michael and his wife gave themselves completely to Jesus. In a very short time many wonderful changes occurred in their lives. In just a few days time, even their look was different. They were changed and restored. They were able to recover their social status and their personal courage. The two of them went through the complete process of consolidation, but they each felt that they had a great debt towards God and decided to make an effort to please Him in everything. After having finished their studies in the School of Leaders, they decided, as a couple, to offer their service to God for six days a week and work only one day to cover their expenses.

This commitment turned out to be something truly miraculous because on that one day that they dedicated to business, God gave them their provisions for the whole week. The Lord began to bless this couple with many souls, and they began to form disciples. Today, they both have succeeded in increasing their ministry in a great way and their disciples love them! When Michael hears someone say to him, "Man of God, could you lead me in prayer for this need that I have," he feels a great pleasure within his heart for the miracle that the Lord did in his life.

HAVING A CORRECT SELF-IMAGE

Have you ever heard the name Mephibosheth? Let me tell you that he is not some singer or musician but rather someone who was hurt deeply in his life and began to think that he was a mistake, even though he was the grandson of a king, King Saul. Saul was the first king of Israel, but because of disobedience, he and his children all died on the same day. Mephibosheth was five years old when the maid heard the news of the deaths. In all of the bitter excitement she was running hysterically and tripped, causing the boy to fall down and severely damage both of his feet. This accident left the boy lame from that day on. This misfortune left a mark in that child's life, leaving him feeling much abandonment. His father, his uncles, and his grandfather were all dead, and he was crippled. Anyone would think that such a life has no meaning. But what happened in the life of this child has become the voice of nourishment for many people.

KNOWING MERCY

When David had already become king of Israel, he wanted to be merciful to Saul's house. They told him about a grandson of the former king named Mephibosheth, who was also the son of Jonathan, David's friend. The first thing that the king said to him was, "Do not be afraid because I will surely show you mercy for the sake of your father Jonathan, whom I love. I will give back to you all of the land of your grandfather Saul, and you will always eat at my table." The boy humbled himself and asked, "Who is your servant that you look at a dead dog like me?" (2 Samuel 9:7-9)

This act is an illustration of God's Grace. David is a prototype of His grace as it is poured out on each one of us, offering us dignity when we feel that we are not worth anything.

THE MERCY OF GOD TRANSFORMS

I remember a time at one of the men's encounters when I was contemplating the faces of some of the men. I saw their inward conditions affected their outward appearance. It was obvious that failure had always been a part of their lives. But I knew that if they came to understand the grace of God, their lives would change in a radical way. When we taught on repentance and later had a time of ministry, they were then able to effectively carry their own lives to the Cross in an act of faith, which caused them to feel as though they were literally crucified with Christ. For the great majority, this was the first time they had an opportunity to open their hearts without being concerned about the opinions of others around them. When the encounter was over, none of their countenances looked the same. Their faces were glowing; they felt that their doubts had dissipated, their fears had been conquered, their questions had been answered and their burdens had been lifted. Since then the lives of those men, have been transformed and the majority of them have remained in the ministry.

INHERITING THE SPIRIT OF FEAR

"Do not be afraid," were the first words of the king. David could sense that this man had inherited the spirit of fear from his grandfather Saul. God had entrusted Saul with the mission of making war against Amalek, knowing that he should not have mercy on the city because it should have been destroyed in its entirety.

God wanted to use Saul in order to execute justice that had already been declared against the Amalekites. But, because of his fear of the Amalekites, Saul only partially obeyed the divine order, forgiving the better part of the flock and also the life of the king (1 Samuel 15:8-9). The prophet Samuel was so troubled by Saul's disobedience that he told Saul, "Let me declare to you what Jehovah told me." And Saul said, "Tell me." So Samuel continued, "Although you were insignificant in your own eyes, did you not become the head of all of the tribes of Israel? Has God not appointed you the king of Israel?" (1 Samuel 15:16-17).

THE SPIRIT OF FEAR AND LOW SELF-ESTEEM

The whole root of Saul's problem originated from his low self-esteem. Although everyone around him was praising him for his stature, he was already the highest, most handsome person in all of Israel and yet he felt like the most insignificant person in the world. Maybe that is why he felt unworthy to take the life of King Agag or perhaps secretly, Saul admired him. Such feelings opened the door for fear, which ultimately controlled him for the remainder of his life, causing him to take on the behavior that carried him closer and closer to destruction.

Because of this, God left him, and an evil spirit came to torture him. Saul became consumed with jealousy of David, his best leader, and no matter where David went, Saul chased him with the intention of killing him. But God never delivered David into Saul's hands. Instead, the opposite occurred, and David spared Saul on various occasions when he could have taken Saul's life.

King Solomon wisely said, "Fear of man will prove to be a snare" (Proverbs 29:25).

Fear, more than a feeling, is the manifestation of a demonic spirit, but God can set us free from it. That same curse which plagued Saul passed on to his children, who died in battle that same day. But the spirit of fear, inferiority, failure and misery were passed on to be a part of the life of his grandson, Mephibosheth, to whom David extended his mercy so that he would be treated as was due to a king's offspring.

RECEIVING GRACE

"...for I will surely show you kindness for the sake of your father Jonathan" (2 Samuel 9:7).

Grace is the unmerited favor of God shown to each one of us. It is not a payment that people receive for something that they have done. Grace gives people dignity, improves their lifestyle, ensures their family and opens the door so that they may receive many blessing in their lives.

David understood grace very well. When God called him to anoint him, not even his own father, Jesse, took the time to go and pull him out from that place where noone saw him so that he too could stand in line with his brothers as a candidate for this anointing. Jesse saw David as less important than his own brothers. Yet and still, David was chosen and taken from the lone job amidst his sheep, he was anointed and placed as king over the people of Israel in place of Saul, who was removed due to his disobedience. The grace of God comes to our lives even when we feel helpless to stand for ourselves. The apostle Paul said "But God demonstrates his own love for us in this: while we were still sinners, Christ died for us" (Romans 5:8).

I WILL GIVE YOU THE LAND

Even though Mephibosheth was the grandson of a king, he was living as a beggar until David's mercy intervened and he had all of is grandfather's land restored to him. Maybe you are saying, "I cannot receive this because I feel unworthy; I do not deserve it. I have done so many bad things in this life, therefore, someone better than I should receive that favor." On the other hand, you may be saying, "My spiritual leaders taught me that to remain humble I should always live in poverty." But when the favor of God reaches us, God restores His blessings into our lives. "From this day on, I will prosper you!"

DEVELOPING A SUPERNATURAL LEADERSHIP

In other words, the Lord is telling you, "I am restoraing back to you all that the adversary took away from you."

THE ECONOMIC REST

My wife Claudia, and I have always been very happy, but the first six years of marriage we had to pray much for our finances. I was aware of the promises of God in His Word for each of His children, but I saw them as very far off from my life. No matter how hard we tried in our work, we still did not see His blessings.

One day, I said to the Lord "God, I would like to become prosperous. Please help me." Immediately, His Spirit surprised me with a revelation that came to my life: "God made the heavens and earth in six days, and on the seventh day He rested. You have had six years of economic trials. Now you are going to enter the seventh year, the year of rest, and from now on prosperity will come to your home."

In reality, I did not know how this prosperity was going to come, but God showed me later by His great mercy that the whole economic problem was not because of my social status or my work, but because of a demon called *ruin* and that whatever we did was devoured by that demon. My spiritual eyes were opened, and I realized that I was fighting against a spiritual force and that such a battle is won in the spiritual realm. So, I rebuked the spirit of ruin, asking the Lord to renew my mind and when I believed, prosperity came.

You should understand that prosperity comes, not through the business in which you work, or through your own possibilities, but, rather, it comes to your life when you believe it. All the riches of God are within your reach. All you need to do is reach out your hand, take the riches and say, "Lord, I believe that these blessings are for me."

YOU WILL SIT AT MY TABLE

David told Mephibosheth, You will eat bread with me." The Bible says that God is preparing a table for us in the presence of our enemies (Psalm 23:5). God has already prepared a great banquet for each of us. Sit at the table of the Lord and enjoy being in His presence.

Mephibosheth had to come to the table of the king every day. If someone that was invited was not present, it was due to illness or some great tragedy that had occurred. Not under any circumstances, could anyone avoid being at the table of the king, once invited.

In the same way, each of us has received an invitation; the King has invited us to sit at His table, which is to have intimacy with God through prayer. He longs to see our faces every day. We have been called to His table, and we can talk with Him face to face. We can enjoy the abundance of His table and listen to His sweet voice. His voice is not past, nor future. It is for us today!

Mephibosheth did not have anything, but he found grace in the eyes of the king. He was accepted and prospered within the sanctuary of the royal family. Our God is like that. His blessings are real, and He tells us just like a loving father, "No eye has seen, no ear has heard, no mind has conceived what God has prepared for those who love him" (1 Corinthians 2:9).

WHAT DO YOU THINK OF YOURSELF?

"Who is your servant, that you look at a dead dog like me?" (2 Samuel 9:8).

I believe that there is nothing sadder than when a person comes to feel that he or she is something despicable and everyone else feels like he or she is repulsive as well. One of the most repugnant things to the human nostril is the strong, stinking smell of a dead dog. The fact that Mephibosheth used this comparison to identify with, showed the deplorable spiritual and emotional state, in which he found himself in. A person in such a circumstance loses the spirit of conquest and accepts the idea that he is a failure. Mephibosheth began to accept that idea, perhaps because of people around him. Even though he was the grandson of a king and was in a good economic position, he began to believe that his life was a complete mistake due to his physical condition (a cripple) and the atmosphere in which he lived. That idea of being a dead dog could not have come from God. So then, where does it come from? The enemy plants thoughts in people's minds like seeds.

The best ground in which such seeds will germinate is in the lives of people who have been beaten up by different adversities or exposed to great tests. The fire of an ordeal either results in purification or has a consuming effect. People either draw nearer to God and give Him the glory or, on the contrary, fall into depression and hope to die.

WHAT CAN YOU DO WHEN THERE IS NO HOPE FOR LIVING?

A couple that attends our church made a visit to the doctor regarding a muscular problem that the husband was having only to have the doctor say to him, "Make all the necessary preparations because you will not survive this week. You might even pass away by tomorrow." Imagine the emotional state that the couple found themselves in. You can imagine that they felt like the world was falling in on them.

In such moments, people are generally open to receive seeds of the word of God, or the deception of the enemy. In situations like these, some people begin to think that God has failed them and that all of their devotion to Him was a waste of time. If the enemy succeeds in convincing people to believe this idea, he gains ground in their lives. But if we believe the promises of God and cling on to them, declaring them with all of our hearts, we know that the Lord will extend His mercy, and we will see truly extraordinary miracles.

That couple decided to believe God. I met with them that same day and I took authority over the spirit of sickness, rebuking it in the name of Jesus. The couple went home very joyful, resting on the promises of God. During that week in which the doctor said that the husband would die, he completely recovered his health. That was more than fifteen years ago. Today, they both minister as pastors, and are powerfully blessed by God.

The interesting thing that I like to emphasize is how David did not treat Mephibosheth according to how he felt, but rather, he treated him in the same special way as if he was one of his own children (2 Samuel 9:11).

Chapter 9

TEACH THEM THAT THEY HAVE INHERITED BLESSING

"I will make you into a great nation and I will bless you;
I will make your name great, and you will be a blessing."

Genesis 12:2

A WATCH IN GOD'S HANDS

When we listen to the word inheritance, we think about material goods that may have passed from one generation to other; but there is an inheritance that is much more valuable than this it is the inheritance of the blessing. To be participants of this blessing we have to fulfill certain requirements that for God are indispensable, such as loyalty, respect, commitment, obedience and the detaching of things that can be an obstacle in our lives.

We can grasp the ministry, our reputation or some material good. It is very easy to speak out, from our lips, that we love God and that we are ready to give Him everything that He asks of us. But when He demands it, we get confused thinking, Lord, you would never ask me for that. This is not God talking to me; it must be my imagination.

That which you love the most is what God will ask you for. The Lord asked me a question in a moment when we were flowing as a church in a very special time of worship. The glory of God had fallen, and I found myself on the floor worshiping the Lord. In that moment, the Lord asked me this question, "Of everything that you have, what is it that you love the most?"

"The ministry," I told Him.

Then He asked me, "If you were to lose your ministry, would you give it to me?"

I responded, "Yes, Lord. Everything that you ask of me is yours."

Then He asked, "Of all of your possessions, which do you love the most?"

Then I understood where the Lord was guiding me to. I told him, "The watch." That watch had been bought for me by a friend, at a special price because he wanted me to have it. He told me that it was a collectible and that if I were to find a similar one, its price would not be less than $25,000. I thought that my friend was exaggerating, but when I gathered some information, I was able to verify what he had said. My appreciation for the watch changed when I knew its true value. Then, it became my Isaac. God realized that I loved it too much. The following day when we were worshiping again, the glory of God fell upon me and soon I heard a voice say to me, "I want the watch." I was so surprised by such words that I automatically thought that it was my own imagination. I responded, "Lord, I take authority, and I bind this thought."

After a while, again, I heard the words, "I want your watch." I thought that it had something to do with the atmosphere. I began to feel as though I was getting some strange sensory perception that was affecting my thought process. It was not easy for me to accept that but in reality, God was asking for my Isaac.

Again I heard the voice, "Are you going to give me the watch or not?" Then I exclaimed, "Oh, Lord, it is your voice! Take the watch, it is all yours."

Later, He showed me the person to whom I should give it to, it was one of the speakers at the conference. When I got close to him and gave him the watch, this brother stared at me in great surprise and asked me, "Why this?"

I answered, "Take it as a gift from the Lord."

Three years later, we were in the church worshiping the Lord when the power of God fell and I heard His voice say to me, "My child, do you remember that watch?"

I responded, "How could I forget it?"

Then he answered me, "Let me teach you something: if you had not given me that watch, I would have asked you for the ministry."

At that moment, I almost collapsed. That day, I understood that the watch did not have any value compared to the ministry. God was testing me in something very small, and if I had not been faithful in that, I would have lost the bigger thing, the ministry. God tests us in small things before entrusting us with big things (Matthew 25:21), and He tests us in the material before He entrusts us with the spiritual.

THE GOD OF ABRAHAM

Abraham is a perfect example of what a true father is as succeeding in raising up a generation for God. God Himself told Moses, "Say to the Israelites, 'the LORD, the God of your fathers—the God of Abraham, the God of Isaac and the God of Jacob—has sent me to you.' This is my name forever, the name by which I am to be remembered from generation to generation" (Exodus 3:15)

"The Lord had said to Abram, 'leave your country, your people and your father's household and go to the land that I will show you. I will make you into a great nation, and I will bless you. I will make your name great, and you will be a blessing. I will bless those who bless you, and whoever curses you I will curse; and all peoples on earth will be blessed through you'" (Genesis 12:1-3).

Abraham represents faith and has become the father of faith. God was so pleased with the life of this man that he decided to make an eternal covenant with him and with his descendants. If we take his example, we should understand that God demands that we have a certain degree of faith so that he can make a covenant with us and with our disciples. For that to become a reality; He must first clean out the different areas of our lives where we may have been contaminated. He'll do this by guiding us through a deep process of sanctification until every spiritual value is alive again.

HEIRS OF BLESSING

The land that He wants to give to us to possess is the land of biblical promises that He has prepared for us and for our disciples. But in order to conquer them, we must have the same spirit of faith that Abraham had. Abraham believed God, which was counted for him as justice, and he came to be a friend of God. Abraham believed in hope against hope; he placed all of his confidence in God, and by this faith he did not stop to look at his circumstances. His human hope was very weak because of all of the circumstances that were against him, but he learned to strengthen himself in God and to call things that do not exist as though they were (Romans 4:17-18). Abraham not only believed in his mind but he confessed with his mouth and made use of the power of the spoken word. He spent whole nights staring at the stars and calling to his descendants. He not only saw the faces of his descendants but he also gave them names.

By this confession, he was able to give life to entire nations. People that are closest to the heart of God are those who have the ability to believe.

DECIDE TO WALK ON THE PATH OF FAITH

This was the only way that Abraham could please God and come to be a participant in His divine nature. This life of faith opened the doors for him and showed him the path that would lead him to success.

Faith gave him the strength to overcome all the obstacles that he found in his life. Faith became the bridge that helped him to cross the abyss of separation that was between the possible and the impossible.

FAITH REJUVENATES

Through faith, Abraham and Sara could drink from the spring of life that rejuvenated them and made them vigorous, so much that a king wanted to take Sara as a wife, who was over seventy five years old.

If Sara existed in our days, she would be one of the women most requested to share the formula of the eternal youth.

VISION OF THE CELESTIAL CITY

Also he could fly wrapped in the wings of the Spirit. He crossed the celestial city, whose architect and builder is the same God. With this revelation he was able to keep his eyes on the promise.

HIS OFFSPRING

By that same faith, Abraham also left a blessing for his offspring. Since Christ is the seed of Abraham, if we are in Christ, we are certainly part of the lineage of Abraham and heirs of the promise.

SAW HIS DESCENDANTS

The promises that God gave Abraham are also for us, and only by faith in His Word can we fulfill each one of our promises also given to our patriarch. In the same way, Abraham successfully imprinted on his mind the clear images of his descendants. With the same faith, we can also give life to those pictures that we have successfully imprinted in our hearts. Whatever a person successfully paints with the pencil of faith here on earth, will be accepted by God in heaven because aside from our physical eyes, God has also given us spiritual eyes. If we succeed in developing our spiritual vision, we will be able to see clearly that the greatest miracles are done by

God Himself. As the Apostle Paul said, "So we fix our eyes not on what is seen, but on what is unseen. For what is seen is temporary, but what is unseen is eternal" (2 Corinthians 4:18).

Once we succeed in determining, with clarity, the miracle that we need to conquer, seeing it clearly in our hearts, we only have to speak the word with authority, so that it will be reproduced in the natural exactly as we have visualized it to be. Everything that we succeed in visualizing in the spiritual world will become a great reality in the natural world. The spiritual always comes before the natural.

DEPENDING TOTALLY ON GOD

If you let faith grow in your heart, you will be surprised at the things that you will be able to believe and conquer. The word of faith houses so much power that the things that seem impossible are reached and conquered through it. If it is so important, why aren't more people concerned with having it?

The life of faith demands absolute dependence on God an many people struggle with this because they want to receive honor for their successes. But in the world of faith, the glory for the greatest deeds falls exclusively on God.

We only come to be participants of the divine nature when we throw ourselves into walking down the path of faith. Whoever does not walk by faith cannot please God.

THE GOD OF ISAAC

Isaac represents the promise. God had promised that a generation would be called forth from within Isaac. Isaac is a prototype of the children whom God gives. Something that we have experienced in the ministry is that those spiritual children whom we have successfully conceived in prayer have become as close to us as our own children are. In the same way that Isaac brought laughter, those who we have conceived spiritually bring a great satisfaction to our lives. Isaac received all of the benefits of his father; He equally enjoyed the spiritual, as well as the material, lot that his father left for him. If we could define the life of Isaac in concise terms, it would be thought of as the: casting off that which we love the most. Of all of the tests that Abraham endured, God's request for him to sacrifice his son, became the most difficult.

A UNIQUE TESTIMONY

When we returned from a three-day couple's encounter, there was a reception in a hotel consisting of family members of those who attended the encounter. One of the men took the opportunity to testify about what God had done for him in those three days. Although he was very new in the Christian life, he was very excited as he recounted the miracle in his marriage. But by the way he was testifying, it was obvious to me that there was something from his past life that he still had not released. He and his wife had children, but there were only sons born to this union. For eighteen years he had been carrying on an affair with another women and the birth of a little girl was the result of it. Since that time, the life of this man was parted in two because he loved his family, but he also felt responsible for the other woman and her daughter. The testimony that he gave went like this: "Dear friends, for eighteen years I had an extramarital affair and we had a daughter, but in this encounter I was able to renounce that woman—the mother of my daughter. Even though she has been a very good woman and has always taken good care of my daughter, she has sacrificed and suffered a lot. I kept both relationships for many years, but in this retreat I decided to renounce her."

It was easy to see that the heart of this man was still connected to the heart of that woman. Claudia and I felt sorry for his wife while he was testifying because we saw that for him, the good, sacrificing woman was not his wife, but rather the other woman.

LET GO OF THE PENNY

After the meeting was over, I called him aside wanting to help him understand his mistake. I began with an illustration: "One time, a child was playing with a penny that fell inside of a vase. Although it was wide inside, the top part was quite narrow. When the child wanted to get the penny out of the vase with his fist closed, his hand would not fit through the opening. The child began to yell, "Daddy, daddy, my hand is stuck in the vase." The father came to him, looked at him and said, "Son, it is very simple; you just have to open your hand and you can take it out without any problem."

The child quickly responded, "Daddy, if I open my hand the penny will fall out."

So the father took out a bill of money from his wallet and said to the child, "Son, this is worth more than the penny. Open your hand, and I'll give you the bill." But the child repeated, "No, I want my penny." Later, I told this man, "By the testimony that you shared I see that you still have not released the penny because your life is still very much akin to the life of that woman. If you make the decision to let go of the relationship, God has prepared a better blessing for your life, and you will be able to redeem the time that you have denied to your wife and to your children." Although it took him awhile to cast that relationship from his heart, he was finally able to do it. Today, he and his family serve the Lord within the church, and God has used them a lot in marital counseling.

In general, God asks us for everything that hinders our life and ministry, but when He does it, it produces a change in our lives because God transforms our weaknesses into strengths and uses that which shamed us, to bless others.

THE GOD OF JACOB

Jacob and Esau were fighting ever since they were in Rebecca's womb, perhaps over who would be born first. Esau was born first, but Jacob was born grabbing his brother by the heel. Esau was reddish, so he was given the name Edon, which means red, while they gave his brother the name Jacob, which means he who grasps the heel or supplants. When he was born, Jacob was at a disadvantage in relation to his brother because his parents had already passed through to their destiny, and had not given Jacob the better part. So, the name supplanter was not much different than usurper, which is why Isaac turned his heart towards the older brother from the beginning.

THE NAME DETERMINES THE DESTINY

A couple from our congregation had a daughter who was born prematurely after only six months. For several weeks, she was in an incubator, but the child remained inflamed and swollen. They called her Emily. She improved very slowly. The situation was very difficult. The father went to the clinic every day and watched over her.

He gave her words of encouragement such as, "Emily, you are going to be fine. Emily, you are a blessing. My Emily, the Lord is going to heal you." Even though he was speaking to the little girl, she showed no signs of improvement.

One day, he decided to investigate the meaning of her name. To his surprise, it means inflamed and swollen. He said, "My God, forgive me for having given that name to my daughter." That was why the girl experienced no improvement because the dad was saying every day, "My inflamed and swollen one, how are you? My inflamed and swollen one, the Lord is with you." After receiving this revelation, he renounced that name and changed it to Valentina, which means made an effort and valiant. The same day that he began to call her Valentina, the inflammation and swelling went down and she began to improve. The pediatrician told the father, "This is the first case that I know of where the change of a name transformed a baby for the better."

JACOB, AND THE BIRTHRIGHT

Each time that someone called him or greeted him, he remembered that he was the one who seizes by the heel bone. Jacob accepted that as his nature. Jacob took advantage of the moment when his brother was hungry in order to buy the birthright from him. To be the firstborn was the equivalent of being the legal heir of the family, and it was conferred on whomever received the blessing for the descendants. God should be known as the God of Abraham, of Isaac and Esau, but since Esau sold his birthright for a bowl of soup, God would be remembered as the God of Abraham, of Isaac, and of Jacob. You have a birthright; that right is obtained when you give your heart to Jesus and become a child of God.

HE VALUED THE BLESSING

When Isaac was an old man, very advanced in age and felt that his time on this earth was growing short, he decided to give the inheritance of the blessing that he had received from Abraham, his father, to his son Esau. But, Jacob shrewdly replaced his brother and took the whole blessing in his stead. His father went on to blessed him: "So he went to him and kissed him. When Isaac caught the smell of his clothes, he blessed him and said, «Ah, the smell of my son is like the smell of a field that the LORD has blessed. May God give you of heaven's dew and of the earth's richness and abundance of grain and new wine. May nations serve you and peoples bow down to you. Be lord over your brothers, and may the sons of your mother bow down to you. May those who curse you be cursed and those who bless you be blessed» (Genesis 27:27-29).

Later, Esau implored his father to bless him too, but there were no more blessings. Although he insisted, the blessing that he obtained was this: "Your dwelling will be away from the earth's richness, away from the dew of heaven above. You will live by the sword and you will serve your brother. But when you grow restless, you will throw his yoke from off your neck" (Genesis 27:39-40).

THE BLESSING IS MUCH CLOSER THAN THE CURSE

Because of this, Esau swore that after his father died he would kill his brother. Jacob had to flee for fear of his brother. Years later, Jacob received news that his brother was coming to meet him. Esau was planning to avenge because of the built up resentment that he had for his brother. That night Jacob was very anxious because he knew that his brother was coming to take vengeance and that four hundred men were coming with him. Jacob foresaw the danger because he felt oppression in the spiritual world. He made his family cross over a ford, leaving him alone. During this time, a man appeared to him and shortly thereafter, he began to wrestle with the man, which actually turned out to be an angel. In Jacob's desperation he fought with all his might, ignoring the angel's insistence for Jacob to release him. Jacob refused to do it until the angel blessed him. Jacob knew that the curse was coming full speed ahead to meet him. But he also knew that the angel was a personification of God; He was the only one who could change the circumstances.

THE BLESSING IS VERY CLOSE TO YOU

We can understand that the blessing is closer than the curse; we simply must persevere and appropriate it to make it ours. That night, Jacob began to look at the countenance of the angel. As he contemplated it, he understood the change because through the countenance of the angel he could see clearly that all of the circumstances were transformed. He knew that his brother would no longer be angry or full of vengeance. He could see that the whole cloud of demons that were moving, working and oppressing the mind of his brother, broken by the power of God. And angels were coming with thoughts of peace, forgiveness and reconciliation.

BLESSING CHANGES YOUR NAME

The first angel asked Jacob, what is your name? Later, the man said to him, you will no longer be called Jacob (supplanter) but Israel (Prince of God), because you have struggled with God and with men, and you have overcome.

WE ARE TRANSFORMED IN HIS PRESENCE

The life-changing experience of that night was reflected in the following day, when Jacob had to meet his brother, Esau. He told him, "For to see your face is like seeing the face of God, now that you have received me favorably" (Genesis 33:10b).

In order for Jacob to be able to become a spiritual man, he had to experience a breakthrough in prayer that separated his spirituality and his human nature. Only God can do that when there is firm determination to serve Him according to His guidelines. Just as a caterpillar has to release its old nature in order to become a butterfly, each believer has to release everything that is a hindrance to his or her spiritual development. In his letter to the Corinthians, Paul helps us to understand that every believer should have such an experience. "And we, who with unveiled faces all reflect the Lord's glory, are being transformed into his likeness with ever-increasing glory, which comes from the Lord, who is the Spirit" (2 Corinthians 3:18). Notice that the measure in which we are in the presence of God, determines our transformation where God helps us to release those attitudes that have caused flaws in our character. This can only be achieved with the help of the Holy Spirit of God.

JACOB AND THE GOVERNMENT OF THE TWELVE

Jacob represents the government of the twelve. From Jacob, the people of God were consolidated into twelve tribes. However God had to work diligently in his life and character, so that the blessing could later be extended through each of his children. It was through the twelve that the great multiplication came like the stars in the heavens and as multitudes.

Chapter 10

FORM DYNAMIC LEADERS

"Well done, good and faithful servant. You have been faithful with a few things; I will put you in charge of many things."

-Matthew 25:21

Getting involved and being part of the ministry is one of the greatest honors that any human being can have. Nothing compares to it. No other kind of success, however great it may seem — be it professional, personal, or financial — ever exceeds the honor of being called to the ministry. When we know the heart of God, it will be easier for us to understand the Mission that He has entrusted us with here on this earth. But He first tests us before placing us into the ministry. Each one of us is like a diamond in the rough, we need to go through the whole process.

A few days ago, a friend told me about the process of refining a diamond. Knowing the four-step process for this precious stone really got my attention. I saw a great parallel between the process that my friend described and what God has to do with those whom He calls to ministry:

1. Cutting.
2. Polishing.
3. Finding the best possible clarity.
4. Mounting the stone in a high place where it can receive light from above and below.

CUTTING THE DIAMOND: BROKENNESS

The experts at cutting diamonds are the Jews. The expert in broken hearts is the Lord Jesus. God knows when people are turning their hearts away from Him. There are many people who begin their Christian lives with a tender heart, but the lights of this world attract them and lead them away from the divine purpose. In such cases, the Lord must intervene and deal with those hearts so that those lives will not be lost.

If Joseph had not remained faithful when he was tempted by Potiphar's wife (Genesis 39), he may have never come to be the great man who lead the nation of Egypt. God always tests us in small things. Everyone who is in the ministry should be tested in one way or another. God gives each person a small or a large ministry according to the response to the test. Almost everyone who is in the ministry has a great desire to please God, in the area that He has entrusted the person with, but some are tempted to abandon everything when they face many obstacles in their path. This would be a great triumph for the enemy because he desires to stop everyone who is winning souls for Jesus. We should understand that the Lord allows us to be attacked by the adversary, who can come with different kinds of tests, but God uses these tests to form us.

Brokenness is the university through which God allows us to pass so the likeness of Christ would be formed in us. "If a grain of wheat does not fall into the earth and die it remains alone, but if it dies it will bear much fruit." It would not serve any purpose for us to be like beautiful grains, diligent in our spiritual duties, or lead a normal family life if we have not been broken. This is the only way to be born into a new life in Him. No one wants to go through tests and difficulties, but God uses adversity to mold our character.

When we went to Italy, we visited Venice. While we were there, we took a tour to an Island where Murano crystal is made. One of the workers showed us the process of how they make it. They put the crystal in an oven at very high temperatures, and the crystal begins to burn as if it were a ball of fire. Then, they take it out of the oven and it gets formed into the desired shape, in a matter of seconds. I realized then that something similar happens when Christians go through difficult times. This was likened to the fiery furnaces in which we are tested. Sometimes God allows a hopeless situation so that we would submit our pride, set aside our self-confidence, and open ourselves to Him saying, "Take my life and do with it whatever you want." When we reach that point, we are like the crystal that has just been taken out of the furnace, and the Holy Spirit can come and shape us however He desires to.

We should understand that the greatest experiences come out of the greatest adversities: a test with our children, a sickness, an economic crisis, a marital conflict, etc. In the hands of God, these tests are transformed into great blessings. Or, we might ask, does adversity indicate that God has failed us? Nothing could be further from the truth. It is necessary to go through tests in order to understand that God wants to take us to a new level of faith that will help us to mature. Maybe you are asking yourself, "Why have I been going through different tests for so long?" The answer is very simple: God wants you to be a precious jewel who has been shaped after Jesus´s character. God wants to carry you to a new level of faith where you flow continually in His blessing. You are a beautiful diamond that God is shaping.

GOD'S DEALING WITH THE LEADER (POLISHING THE DIAMOND)

In order for the diamond to have that special characteristic of luster on each facet, it should be polished. What is it that the Holy Spirit does in people's lives? He polishes them. He deals with them until He smoothes out the rough places in their hearts. He then displays them so that they can shine in every facet of their lives.

When God spoke to me about the ministry, He gave me the order of priorities that I should have.

1. *"I must always be the first in your life"*. Many people believe in God, but they don't live their lives centered in His love. The Lord showed me that I should live my life as an expression of my deep love for Him. It is not enough to believe in Him; even the demons believe in Him and shake in fear (James 2:19). God wants us to have a passionate love relationship with Him, one in which we love Him with all of our minds, all of our souls, and all of our strength (Deuteronomy 6:5) so from the moment we open our eyes we tell Him that we are in love with Him. He wants us to feel His presence every time we breathe. He wants us to have a deep intimacy with Him that is not religious but is a relationship with the Spirit of God. Many people have been unable to have such a relationship with the Holy Spirit due to a religious spirit.

2. *"Your life is important"*. Your life is the channel through which the Holy Spirit flows. We should take great care of our bodies, our minds, our emotions, our feelings all of our being. We are instruments, weapons in the hands of God. But in order for Him to use us, He needs our lives to be sanctified and consecrated in His holiness.

3. *"Your family should be a model"*. God showed me that we should not have just any kind of family, but that He wants us to have the best family in the whole world. This

meant that I must love my wife and children with all of my heart. I must be an example for them and always esteem them highly—even more than the ministry.

When we celebrated Father's Day, my third daughter wrote me the following note: *"Daddy, I see that we have always had a very important place in your heart. Thanks for putting your family ahead of the church. If you have to leave any church activity for us, you do so. Thanks for the way you teach us these things because you and my mother are an example for each of us."*

Although we as Christian leaders have the great responsibility to reach the nations of the earth with the gospel of Jesus Christ, we sometimes forget that we have families. And what purpose is there if people get saved in other nations but your family is lost?

I remember on one occasion in which God made this point more clear to me. It was a little after we had started our church in Miami, and we had about 200 members. I arrived at our Sunday meeting at ten o'clock in the morning. Only about 30 brothers were there, and I began to feel disappointed because I was accustomed to seeing multitudes of our church in Bogota. And there, as discouragement was starting to build up in me, I began to worship. As I did, I saw my daughter Lorena leading worship. I saw my daughters Manuela and Sara leading dances. And I saw my daughter Johanna ministering to some youth. At that moment, I felt the Lord's presence, and I saw how blessed I was to have my family there. So I said "Thank you, Lord. If there was no one in this place but my daughters, I would still thank you because each one of them is worth hundreds of thousands of people to me." That morning, I thanked the Lord because my family serves Him.

Dear friend, God has entrusted you with your first cell group: your family. If you cannot save your family, how is He going to trust you with the nations? God wants to restore families. Why do pastors divorce in the United States? It is because the family does not have a major role within the ministry. We must go back to the beginning of what the Lord taught us and give family the place that it deserves.

4. *"Your ministry"*. Although family comes before ministry, it is important to understand that we must motivate the family that we are raising, primarily with our example, so that they will also get involved in the ministry. I know that in these last days, God is bringing a great spiritual awakening to entire families where, unlike in the past, they are not becoming passive members of their communities but rather there is a great enthusiasm in all of them to extend the Kingdom God.

5. *"Secular work"*. For many people, these priorities are in a different order because they put work, not only in first place, but in second and third place, too. In order to fulfill their financial obligations, some people have three jobs, which takes up all their time. They can only give a few minutes to their families, and they put God in last

place. We should understand that work is important, but when it takes the first place in our life there is a significant spiritual and physical consequence. Because of this, your family and ministry will suffer.

KEEP THE PURITY OF THE VISION (THE CLEARNESS OF THE DIAMOND)

Some people are just satisfied with only a vague idea of God's vision. You cannot be one of them. The first thing that you have to understand is that this vision is based on the scripture. When I talk about the vision, I am referring to the government of the Twelve, which is the Holy Spirit's strategy for this time. It stimulates the growth of churches and allows each believer to fulfill the purpose of God throughout the earth. Each pastor and leader who desires to grow in his ministry should become an expert in this vision. You must immerse yourself in it and not allow anything to confuse, pollute, or dilute it.

AVOID TAKING SHORTCUTS

I have observed that some people want to take shortcuts in accomplishing the vision, but we cannot allow this. When we started the Church in Miami, I wanted to take a shortcut myself. Even though I am supposed to know and understand the vision, we all look for shortcuts. I told myself one day, "The easiest way to fulfill the vision in Miami is to take leaders from Colombia. They understand the vision, and they know how to do it." I took several couples who would help in the task, and I told them that they would build the Ministry in Miami. Since they already knew the vision, they would know how to respond in the proper way. They would serve God with excellence. I also thought that by doing this I could protect my name. If they didn't grow, it would be their problem, not mine. But those who came did not adapt well to the lifestyle of Miami and said, "Pastor, we want to go back to Bogotá." I gave them permission to do so, and I began to think about other couples that I could send to Miami. That was when the Lord told me that the couple that had to go to Miami was my wife and I. I told Him that could not be so because I already had a lot of ministry work in Bogotá and many commitments that I needed to respond to. God never discusses matters with you; He just gives the command. He spoke to me clearly—first to me, then to my wife and daughters: "Let's go to Miami."

We began to work there with great effort. Then God began to reveal to us the principalities of the city. For a year, we were breaking demonic powers in the air, clearing the heavens in order to bring the blessings of God. We did this until we felt that the church was born, and now it is bearing fruit. God wants to use you to change your city.

APPLY THE VISION

We have to know the depth of the vision and apply it correctly. This means that you have to study the books that we have written about it. We recommend that you teach and apply everything relative to this vision step by step, even though it may seem simple. You cannot avoid or set anything aside. The only ones who have had problems applying the vision are the ones who have not wanted to change the whole traditional structure. On the other hand, those who want to implement it have to set aside everything that they know and apply it just as it is.

Every leader who wants his church to grow and multiply, must work. Remember that the first Christians met every day in the temple and in homes. With this vision, the whole church works every day—and all day—in the church and at home. It is a question of raising up a whole army of men and women who go out to conquer the city. And whenever there is demonic opposition in the air, everyone rises up as mighty warriors and breaks through the air in the name of Jesus.

THE FRUIT GIVES HONOR (MOUNTING THE STONE)

Each person who is involved in ministry will be honored, not for how long they have served but by the fruit that he or she bears for God. In the parable of the talents, the Lord did not reward the servant who neglected his talent by burying it in the ground, only to return to it later, still intact. God honors those who multiply.

BEING FAITHFUL IN LITTLE

We know that the things of God go from the least to the most. Solomon said, it is like the light of the dawn that grows brighter and brighter until the full day.

A ministry does not begin with multitudes. Maybe you picture yourself in the future preaching to multitudes, nevertheless, the scripture teaches that he who is faithful in little is faithful in much. At the beginning, God is not going to give you great responsibilities; He will train you with little tasks. If you are faithful in those little things, God will entrust you with much.

THE PRIVILEGE OF THE CALL

Most people have great dreams. They spend all of their lives trying to fulfill them, but I believe that one of the most satisfying dreams is to be called to the ministry. It is a great blessing to be chosen out of the thousands of millions of people on this planet. There is no greater privilege.

Right now, God needs men and women who are committed in their hearts, minds, souls, and spirits. He needs people who will invest all of their energy into their work. He needs people who can enlarge and establish His reign on this earth.

PROGRESSIVE DEVELOPMENT AND PERMANENT GROWTH

Every minister has the responsibility to develop progressively and have continued growth. We know that there are two dominant forces in this world which are the forces of good and the forces of evil. Specifically, the call is to establish His reign on this earth, beckoning people to break away from evil and to learn to do what is right in the sight of God.

God is calling us to influence our society and give them a different alternative. Living a life of integrity and holiness blesses those around us, cleans the air, activates the angels, makes heaven descend to earth, and changes the atmosphere.

HAVE THE RIGHT ATTITUDE

In order for any ministry to grow, you should have the right attitude. If the leader thinks that it is not going to grow, that is what he will experience. If you plan for something small, that is what you will get. If you do not understand the vision, it will be difficult to implement it. If you believe that the people around you will not commit, they will not commit. However, if you believe that they are going to be the best group of twelve, this is what you will see with time. The leader should have an attitude of faith because ministerial growth comes from within. When the person believes it and overcomes obstacles such as fear and impossibilities, and determines to conquer them, he will win the victory first in his heart and then later the result will become a reality. When you have that capacity to believe, the miracle will happen.

FRUITFUL BRANCHES IN THE HANDS OF GOD

There is a specific time when we must fulfill our goals. Beginning in the year 2001, we met with the team and established goals to be accomplished within a desired time frame. The team worked all year to reach those goals, but when we were almost to the point of reaching them, I realized that the pastors and leaders were very discouraged.

They did not have faith, and they told me, "We are not going to be able to fulfill the goals." I was surprised by what I heard. It did not make sense to me that the people whom I had trained, people in whom I had been imparting faith for years, would be standing there with their heads down saying, "We can't." I understood that this was not something that came from the Spirit and that Satan had come to bombard them in order to hinder them from completing their goals. While I was praying about this, God informed me that Satan had made the leaders believe that they could not reach their goals and that if they believed that diabolic lie, they would not be able to do it.

However, if they rejected that spirit of unbelief, the fear would disappear and they would fulfill their goals just as they had established.

I met with them and released faith over them. Later, I told them, "I do not accept what you were saying. Having worked for fruit, not to be able to collect it at the end of the year, as planned, is to say that our tree is sterile like the one Jesus cursed. But the bible says that the path of the righteous is like a tree planted by streams of living water that bears its fruit in due season; its leaf will not wither and everything it does prospers. This congregation is a leafy tree. It is a fruitful branch. Each ministry is a fruitful branch, and Satan cannot rob us of the fruit." We rebuked the spirit of unbelief in prayer and later something extraordinary happened in the air; the atmosphere changed, and the pastors started to repent. After that, I could see how their faith had grown, how the spirit of unbelief was broken, how hope was revived and that the fruit from that year would not be lost.

REDEEMING TIME

In the day of Nehemiah, he knew that he only had fifty-two days to reach his goal. He worked for that goal day and night. He did not get discouraged; he did not become weak even for one instant until he achieved his goal. The people had to be in a good frame of mind. They had to be united and work day and night together with Nehemiah. The effort that they were making was so great that they did not even take time to change clothes; they only undressed to bathe themselves and then went back to work. Everyone was working towards the goals; no one strayed from the vision. That is how it has to be with each ministry.

If you have not felt the passion for the goal and have left all the weight of that responsibility on one person, it is time to repent because that is sin and souls are being affected. It is impossible to grow in the ministry without clear goals. If you do not have defined goals, you cannot have clear faith. If you get clarity of thought in your heart, you will be able to reach your goals. Everyone who does not have goals lacks direction in his or her ministry and is going to experience physical, emotional, and economic burnout. Such people will feel that everything has been a waste of time.

BUILDING A CELLULAR WALL

Nehemiah had to face all kinds of obstacles in order to be able to rebuild the wall of Jerusalem because the city was in ruins. But the life of this man became an example that motivated the people.

Leaders should understand the importance of always having a good attitude and staying very motivated so that when they talk with their disciples they impart faith. Nehemiah knew that his main challenge was to raise a wall of protection. We are being called to build a wall, a wall of protection, a cellular wall that has to be as long and wide as the city and later extends to our whole nations. This wall is powerful because it makes even the most violent return to the Lord; it makes the skeptics throw themselves at the feet of Jesus.

We need to have a cell group in each block of our city where the truth of Jesus Christ is proclaimed. We need to strengthen the wall with men, women and youth networks, in order to protect families and guard the city and the nation.

PLEASING GOD

We should understand that without faith it is impossible to please God. It is important that you understand that goals are directly related to faith. I suggest that you write down your goals and that you what goals your team has. Then dedicate all of your energy and all of your resources to achieve them. Do not allow a chasm to grow that will hinder you from fulfilling your goal. If you fail in achieving your goals, you will fail in everything planned for the year. Do not set approximate goals, achieve them and go beyond what you have expected. Every athlete has a goal and that is to win. They prepare themselves for competition, and they go with the desire to win.

Paul said, "Many people participate in a race, but only one receives the prize." We should endeavor, making every effort to receive the prize. This is like a marathon; many people are competing shoulder to shoulder to reach a goal, sometimes for as long as 365 days! In a situation like this, you cannot get discouraged in the road. On the contrary, you need to have a new attitude and say, "I can do all things through Christ who strengthens me".

HAVING A CLEAR IMAGE

Acts 2:17 tells about the moment when the apostle Peter, inspired by the Holy Spirit, speaks to the Jews in a prophetic anointing: "'In the last days', God says, 'I will pour out my Spirit on all people.

Your sons and daughters will prophesy, your young men will see visions, your old men will dream dreams.'"

Peter was prophesying what would happen during this time of God's special anointing; the manifestation was to be in visions and dreams. But, this will come as a result of staying quiet in the presence of God. A vision from God is as clear as the image that you see on television; it should be as clear as a photograph that you snapped yourself. But, if you move the camera, the photo will be blurred.

If you doubt the moment of projecting the vision, you are moved by doubt and the image will turn out blurry. God throws out everything that is not clear. You should believe with all your heart that God will give you what He has promised. God acts above your needs until you have succeeded in becoming a visionary. If you look at failure, you will be a failure, but if you look at success, you will be a successful person. You have to learn to move in the dimension of faith. The writer of Proverbs said, "Where there is no vision, the people perish" (Proverbs 29:18). Satan will fight so that you do not have vision, so that you do not have a clear image, so that you do not have goals in your mind because without vision the results will be uncertain.

The Holy Spirit is the One who is in charge of bringing the vision to your mind. You should meditate on it repeatedly, day after day, until your mind has the conviction that the goal has been reached. You should focus until you feel deep inside that you have accomplished it.

The Holy Spirit is the One who enables all to fulfill their visions and dreams, but if you do not look with faith, the Holy Spirit will not have anything to work with when you pray.

Believe, visualize, confess and God will do the miracle. If you see that people do not commit, they will not do it. Have a vision of multitudes, see clearly that you are a leader, and see how the multitudes follow you.

Chapter 11

HELP THEM UNDERSTAND THE IMPORTANCE OF FORMING THE G12

"Upon this rock I will build my church".

Matthew 16:18

A FOUNDATION ESTABLISHED BY GOD

Twelve is the number of government in the divine plan. The church of Christ was formed of living stones, people who had been transformed by His divine power and whose character already showed stability. Jesus announced His plan when he declared "Upon this rock I will build my church" (Matthew 16:18).

The apostle Paul declared that we have been "built on the foundation of the apostles and prophets, with Jesus Himself as the cornerstone" (Ephesians 2:20). In order to develop the vision in a way that would continue through the centuries, the Lord Jesus chose twelve men, and He transformed their lives in those three years of His ministry, making them powerful giants of faith. Those men were able to drink directly from the fountain of wisdom because each word that left Jesus' lips was inscribed on their hearts and was difficult to forget. Christ is the cornerstone, and Jesus raised up the Twelve as pillars of the temple so that they would support the weight of the church.

FINDING THE MISSING PART

Initially, Jesus' group of twelve was incomplete because one of them did not have a right heart. Once Judas was replaced, that became a sign that the church was indeed ready to be built.

The first extraordinary thing that happened to the church after the twelve were complete, was the outpouring of the Holy Spirit over all of those who were gathered. As a result, the church experienced unprecedented growth. After hearing Peter's first message, three thousand people converted to Christianity.

A few days later, two of the disciples went to the temple and because of the healing of a lame man, five thousand more were added to the church. And each day the Lord added those who had been saved because the church was growing and the number of disciples was multiplying in a great way.

ENGRAVE THE VISION IN THEIR HEARTS

The Lord told the prophet Jeremiah that he would do something new with His people: "I will put my law in their minds and write it on their hearts" (Jeremiah 31:33). We have been able to see this in those who have embraced the vision. Once the vision is received in the spirit, it is much easier to implement the method. When the vision enters the heart, it becomes clear that people will read the vision through our lives. Paul said, "You are a letter from Christ, the result of our ministry, written not with ink but with the Spirit of the living God, not on tablets of stone but on tablets of human hearts" (2 Corinthians 3:3, NIV). In the same way that the Spirit of God has written the vision in our hearts, we also should allow the same thing to happen to our disciples.

AUTHORITY WAS GIVEN TO US

Before ascending to heaven, the Lord met His disciples and gave them what is known as the Great Commission: "Then Jesus came to them and said, 'All authority in heaven and on earth has been given to me. Therefore go and make disciples of all nations, baptizing them in the name of the Father and of the Son and of the Holy Spirit, and teaching them to obey everything I have commanded you. And surely I am with you always, to the very end of the age'" (Matthew 28:18-20).

The Lord begins this declaration with a word of confidence: "All authority in heaven and on earth is given to me." Before giving them the responsibility, the Lord makes them understand that He already did the most important part; He cleared a path for them, leaving them maximum authority in the whole universe. And with that authority He sent them out in His name, as ambassadors. He even warned us that we would face demonic adversities, though nothing would harm us: "I have given you authority to trample on snakes and scorpions and to overcome all the power of the enemy; nothing will harm you" (Luke 10:19). The Christian life is a war, an open war against the spiritual forces of evil in high places; we advance not in our own strength but in the name of Jesus.

GET THE WHOLE CHURCH INVOLVED IN THE VICTORY

When we were a group of thirty people, I was praying, "Lord, what is the effective method for making the church grow?" While I was waiting for His response, an amazing thing happened: the Lord directed me to take the church into a time of prayer and fasting. We organized ourselves to have continuous prayer 24 hours a day. We were only a few people, but we did it. Later, we began a chain of fasting, covering each day of the week until the Lord gave us the victory and we accomplished our goal.

I taught the church that they themselves could do an evangelistic work like no one else could because the people who we needed to win were in the businesses, on their various jobs, in the areas where they lived, and in the universities where they studied. Everyone commited to do an evangelistic work. We began to see the results in a short time.

I was filled with great joy to see how they accepted this challenge and began to work. Our goal was to reach 200 people in six months, but we did it in three months. You should train every church member to participate in the work of God. The potential is already inside each member of the congregation, but you have to know how to transmit the message of what you want and what you long for, to them.

TEACH THEM HOW TO CONSOLIDATE

When the Lord gives us souls, we enter another stage—what do we do to keep them? Consolidating is best illustrated by the care that a mother should give to her newborn child. Such care is what a leader should offer to a recent convert. The time that a person is born again and has a personal encounter with Jesus Christ, is considered foundational in his or her formation. Scientists have proven that the first five years of a child's life determine his or her future personality. Experience shows us that as soon as we win someone, we should begin the process of caring for that person the same way that a mother cares for a newborn.

The type of leader that a person will be in the future depends on the kind of care that is received during those first few months. Regrettably, there are many people who think that their work is done when they see people raise their hands to accept Jesus. Believers often think that having brought people to the church and seeing them commit to the Lord absolves them of further responsibility, and they expect the pastor to handle the rest of the process. But the reality is that such a moment is not the culmination of a process but rather a new beginning, a new birth. This is when the real work begins.

HELP THEM TO GROW

The new believer should be protected with special care that assures normal growth. You should feed them the spiritual milk of the Word. Also, they need to feel and receive the warmth of a home; people who make them feel welcome and comfortable can also be the ones who help them obtain the victory over any lingering temptations that they may be battling. If they are going through financial struggles, you need to help them enter into the dimension of faith that conquers it. All of this work is the proper means by which to produce fruit in each one of these precious lives, if we do it right.

Prepare them for the encounter

Once new believers are consolidated and receive the necessary care from their leaders, the next step is to be discipled. To continue the process, we developed something we call a pre-encounter, which prepares them to go to a three-day retreat that we call an encounter. This encounter is essential because it is there that God works directly in the lives of each new believer. The encounter is the equivalent of being alone with God.

Remember when the people of Israel were in Egypt and the Lord anointed Moses? He told Pharaoh, "Let my people go so that they may adore me for three days in the desert" (Exodus 5:1). The encounter is a time to take the people out of their natural environment, for three days, in order to spend a deep intimate time with God. Pharaoh hardened his heart and denied that exodus, but he said that he would let the women go.

"No, everyone must go," Moses replied.

"Well, I will let the men go," said Pharaoh.

"No, everyone must go," Moses insisted.

"Well, I will let the children go," said Pharaoh, "but their goods must stay here."

"No, everyone must go," Moses replied, "and they must go with their goods."

The people of Israel obtained the victory when they were in the desert for three days and saw the glory of God manifest itself in them.

WHAT IS THE PURPOSE OF THE ENCOUNTER?

The encounter has five fundamental steps:

1. *Assuring salvation*

Many people become Christians without going through repentance. Maybe they were born in Christian homes or they simply changed their religion, but they did not go through a process of repentance. Repentance is that deep internal pain that a person feels for having offended God. A man once told me the following story. "I had two sons, three and five years old. One day I took them with me to a town near Bogotá. In a careless moment, as I entered a shop, my sons ran into the street. A vehicle ran over them, and both were killed." Even though it had happened three years earlier, tears filled his eyes as he told me that he would like to go back in time in order to take better care of his children. Although that situation was very sad, I could understand that God demands something similar from us. It is to desire to go back in time in order not to fail him again. It is to say, "Lord, give me another chance; I will not waste it." Where there is no repentance, there is no deliverance, and the same demons will keep attacking.

2. *Ministering inner healing.*

Many people come from devastated homes where they lived through unspeakable childhood traumas. If you can heal their hearts, then you are doing the work of God correctly. What did the Lord say? "The anointing of God is on me because He has sent me, not only to deliver those who were oppressed but also to heal the brokenhearted" (Luke 4:18). The best way to heal hearts is through the restoration of the love of God the Father. Most people put on fortress-like armor to keep others from knowing that they have certain problems, but when they are alone with God, they can open their hearts and receive ministry from Him.

When Jesus looked from the Cross at the heart of his mother who was hurting, He felt compassion for her and called to his beloved disciple, whose heart was also torn apart because his leader and teacher was dying. It was there that the Lord said, "John behold your mother. Mother, behold your son." He chose them as substitutes and both hearts were healed. When ministering to people, it is important to choose a substitute who can help us minister inner healing. This act is indescribably powerful. A man told me, "Pastor, when I chose a person to take the place of my father, something tremendous happened. I never had spoken to him because I was very afraid of him. When I used that substitute, I truly felt that I was with my father. When I opened my heart, I felt that the fear left and now I no longer have fear in my heart towards my father. I felt compassion for him. I could remove all the hatred from my soul."

3. *Ministering deliverance*

Although some people believe that after accepting Jesus they are completely free from any kind of oppression, many Christians find it difficult to maintain a high degree of holiness and they have been battling continuously against a series of internal conflicts. They do not know how to be free. Satan knows each person's weakness and tries to afflict us continuously, to weaken us spiritually and cause us to turn away from a life of faith. But when there is a genuine repentance, the demon leaves and the person is freed by the power of Jesus Christ. We first need to experience repentance in order to teach about it later. If you have not lived it, you cannot teach it. The greatest power for obtaining deliverance is experienced by each person who understands the power of the Cross.

4. *Ministering the in-filling of the Holy Spirit.*

In Ephesians 5:18, Paul talks against getting drunk. Therefore, there is a general tendency to see drunkenness as sin in light of other lesser ills, but not being full of the spirit is just as sinful. When a person has been healed, liberated, and forgiven, it is very easy to be filled with the Holy Spirit.

The Lord said that this is the biblical order, "And these signs will accompany those who believe: in my name they will cast out demons, they will speak in tongues" (Mark 16:17). Realize that the first task is to cast out demons. The church could avoid many problems if it would correctly take into account this biblical order. The correct order is to cast out demons from the people before they are filled with the Holy Spirit.

5. *Teach them The Vision*

At this point of the encounter, people are ready to receive *The Vision*. They no longer see it as a burden; they understand that they are instruments of God to bless others. From the first moment, new people have to feel a great compassion for the lost, which will become evident and influence their family and friends.

After the encounter, people should stay connected through the post-encounter.

THE IMPORTANCE OF THE POST-ENCOUNTER

Experience taught us that after the encounter Satan counterattacks. When Israel left Egypt, the Pharaoh prepared an attack to destroy them. We were not aware of that; we saw how people were transformed, but we lost many people by not taking special precautions and confronting Satan's strategy of counterattacking. About 70% of people who attended the encounters were lost until the Lord revealed it to people on the team, and they began to work on the *post-encounter* as a strategy to resist Satan's attacks. They developed specific topics for new believers regarding the struggles that they would face, such as temptation and desires to return to their old way of living. They were prepared in such a way that new believers would be taught to face every attack of the enemy effectively.

The post-encounter is a brief training period in which we teach people to remain firm even under the pressure of friends and family as they take dominion and persevere in faith in their Christian lives. With a weak post-encounter, you can run the risk that some people may get discouraged and not return. Remember that new believers should be kept highly motivated, and good motivation lasts only a few days.

COMMIT TO THE SCHOOL OF LEADERS

We began to see that a high percentage of those who attended the Post-Encounter felt motivated to enter into better biblical training. That was how we began to disciple them, through the *School of Leaders*.

We did not work on deep theological topics because we understood that God is using lay leaders. Lay leaders are the ones who reproduce the most. If you analyze the early church, its growth came through lay leadership. And in the great spiritual awakenings, the people whom God used have always been lay leaders. We know that if we give such people the basic tools, they can do the work because lay leaders have the capacity to penetrate places that a pastor or a minister would never reach. A lay leader is in business, in the university, in different neighborhoods, in embassies. He is in so many locations where he can easily speak to others. He can reach every sector of society, but our most important concern is to give them the tools in a simple way, which we call the *School of Leaders*, so that they can do the work of God.

The purpose of the *School of Leaders* is to provide doctrinal formation for disciples in order to prepare them for lay leadership. Our goal is not to create theologians, but to give to the lay leader tools that will help them build their ministry until the vision becomes a lifestyle.

BE PART OF A CELL GROUP

During this process, the person has already been connected to a cell group. In such a group, the doors can be opened so that people's family members, friends, and acquaintances can be touched by the gospel too. New members are given the opportunity to relate to others and have direct contact with the leadership. In a cell, they can also experience the touch of God in a new way.

Chapter 12

TEACH THEM TO BE SUCCESSFUL

"Brothers, I do not consider myself yet to have taken hold of it.
But one thing I do: Forgetting what is behind and straining toward
what is ahead..."
-Philippians 3:13

When you have succeeded in forming your group of twelve, you have become one of the Lord's valiant soldiers, part of His army of great conquerors. You have started the right way, and you will never be the same again. God will do tremendous miracles in your life as He elevates you to a position of dignity. This implies that you will no longer be an ordinary enlisted soldier. Instead, you will become a commander with a team under your control. If this is to be so, you must become an expert in the vision. This is a privilege, but the privilege demands responsibility.

Years ago, I asked several members of my pastoral team to hypothetically rate themselves on a scale of 1 to 100 on their level of commitment to the vision.

The response was upwards to 80%. In turn, I had to explain to them what it would mean not to be 100% committed.

When Jesus arrived in the Garden of Gethsemane, His commitment to the idea of redemption was about 80%; the other 20% involved the sacrifice that He would have to make. In that moment, His spiritual eyes were opened and He clearly saw everything that was awaiting Him in the coming hours. He could have asked for the help of more than twelve legions of angels which would have acted quickly but, He did not want to invoke any of His rights. He opted to take refuge in prayer, asking the Father if it were possible to establish some other way to redeem the human race. If there was no other alternative, then He would be ready to do the Father's will and sacrifice His life. With that prayer, Jesus became totally committed.

To be committed entails full dedication, sacrifice, obedience, work and love. The Lord Jesus knew from the beginning that building the church meant that He would have to give His life to rescue many. I admire those of our leadership who decided to serve God and make the effort to implement the vision without worrying about the price to be paid. Because of this attitude, God has given us the best team in the world because none of them have been seeking to establish their own kingdom but rather to make the kingdom of God great. That is why they are all genuine people, without pretense and given to transparency possessing a great spirit of faithfulness. This shows the degree of commitment to the vision. But that is not all. We should also take into account the following aspects:

COMMON SENSE

There is no handbook that explains how to acquire common sense. We obtain common sense by the circumstances that we live everyday. The greatest discoveries that have benefited mankind came out of the soundness of someone's consistency. It is called common sense. We can say that each one of the components implemented into our vision was simply due to commonsensical logic. We call it, common sense.

When we realized that the people who entered our Biblical Institute for training usually left after two years of study and those who remained did not know how to win the world for Christ, we realized that It was Important to establish a quicker and more effective training program for believers. Previously, we would ask church members if they wanted to enroll in our Bible Institute, but this all changed with the new program, because the vision itself led people directly into training. Due to this rapid growth, we have had to rent locations in different areas of the city (buildings, high schools, universities) in order to accommodate the great number of students who continually arrive.

We have taught our disciples that although we have standards, they should always use common sense. For example, in our cell meetings, we tell them to just be sensitive to the Holy Spirit and His guidance. We try to use mostly conversation, teaching and participation in our cell meetings and only use songs in a few exceptional cases because the majority of our cell leaders do not have that talent.

HELP YOUR DISCIPLES FORM THEIR TWELVE

In the spiritual realm, the result of helping your disciples find and establish their twelve is because of authority, government and maturity. Consider the case of Abraham. Although God promised to make a great nation from his descendants, this promise was not fulfilled until the twelve tribes of Israel were established. Think about the twelve apostles. As I stated in chapter 1, the Lord commissioned them and sent them to do miracles, but the breakthrough did not happen until Judas was replaced and the twelve were complete. The awakening of the people of Israel will be through the anointing of the twelve thousand leaders of each of their tribes.

The Psalmist David said, "God, my times are in your hands." God's watch has twelve numbers also, and through them, He directs our destinies. It is important that each leader teaches his disciples to pursue deep growth. Your goal is not to have a team of twenty or thirty but to prayerfully select your twelve. If one of your leaders is not bearing fruit, you should examine the situation to see where he is failing. He might be very negative with his disciples, or very sarcastic, or unreliable. Maybe when he teaches people, he does it without the anointing; perhaps it sends them into despair!

Generally, in a group of twelve, there are always three that stand out. Nonetheless, it is very important that we help the other ones to form their teams and involve them into the ministry, as well. I know that to form the first group of twelve is quite a feat, but if we are very dedicated to teach the disciples how to follow the process of the vision precisely, they will see positive results in a short time.

My wife became quite an expert at this. She took a group of women with no experience in leadership and dedicated herself to them in a special way. In a matter of about nine months, the results were extraordinary. Although It took her a lot of time, she had the satisfaction of seeing those leaders produce the fruit of her labor.

SINGLE-MINDED FOCUS

The apostle Paul said, "One thing I do..." (Philippians 3: 13). One of the greatest problems in leadership is that there are so many fronts to cover that we often try to take care of all of them and end up neglecting the most important ones.

The first priority for a leader who wants to establish a group of twelve is to concentrate specifically on one cell group.

It is better to have one good group than to have five mediocre ones; the latter approach just reduces your energy level. If you dedicate yourself to one cell group, it will bring to you the people who are ready for an encounter. The best soil for planting the seeds of your vision, for a group of twelve, will be found in a good cell.

A BALANCED LIFESTYLE

We realize that developing this vision demands a lot of time. In our cases, our schedules always conflicted with our kids' schedules, even though they had Saturdays free. But, Saturdays coincided with ministry activities. So then, we had Mondays free, a day when the kids were studying. Then the Lord showed us that they were always home by four o'clock in the afternoon to start studying. Therefore, we decided to be home every day from four o'clock to six o'clock to meet the needs for constant communication between parents and children. Thanks to that decision, our daughters never thought that the ministry competed with them but rather they understood that they themselves were being developed within the ministry.

We cannot let the ministry become a burden. If this happens, it is because something is not being done right. Then, it is necessary for the Lord to reveal to us, in prayer where we are failing. Then, afterwards, we have to correct whatever is necessary so that the Holy Spirit can come into our lives and flow over the leadership that we are exercising.

HOMOGENEOUS GROUPS

Having discovered that home ministry, through the government of the twelve, contributed to spreading the gospel of Jesus Christ in a more effective way, it served to verify that this same process would lead the church towards constant growth, and also make a big impact. However, in order to attain maximum effectiveness from working in this manner, the Lord lead us to look for better results; we looked to more ambitious goals for growth by rearranging the strategy; now, we would begin to measure the affinity among various members of the congregation.

In the beginning the participants of a cell group were not separated by age or gender or regular activities, The cell groups were simply heterogeneous, leaving the cell leader bearing the posture of a hunter who had to shoot at different targets each meeting time! He had to have a word for the men, another word for the women, another word for the young people, another word for the children, another word for couples, and yet another word for new people. Because of that, the results were not optimal.

When we reorganized the cell system by way of the leadership, our focus changed to winning people of the same genre. With regards to this change, we experienced much growth. Some of the pastors took a while to put this into practice, though. Due to having become specialists on preaching to the women, they had to leave all of that responsibility in the hands of their wives and they could focus on winning only men, now. It was something that redirected them to renewing their minds, their faith and their love for a new challenge. Today, we all thank God because, due to this change, their wives have grown much in the ministry, and they have conquered an area that they previously thought would be difficult to do. They have realized that homogeneous groups generate the most increase. This makes the work easier for us because the topics that are discussed are of greater interest to the group.

WORKING WITH GOALS

When you have an objective, the goals are clear. When your objectives are blurred and your goals are not defined, the results are meager. Success is not the result of chance, good luck, or the degree of intelligence that a person has. No! Success comes when people undoubtedly understand the vision. The vision carries you to a purpose, and the purpose directs you to have a specific objective. The specific objective is translated into short-term goals, then long-term goals. These goals will pave the way to elaborate on a plan of action, e.g.

1. To have concrete goals for the following month.
2. To complete that monthly goal (there should be established goals in every area within the vision).
3. For the encounters:
   try to concentrate on having a minimum of 100 people attending each encounter.
4. Help organize them through their networks (support them, teach them, encourage them until they obtain such a degree of maturity that they can lead their own encounters and can reach the goal of having an average of 70 people per encounter).

WIN THROUGH YOUR CELL GROUPS

One important goal is that each cell group should win at least one new person each month. Such a goal would produce a growth rate of three people each quarter, and that cell group should commit to take care of those new people. The cell group is going to help each new member to grow, going through the whole process of the vision, until the new member becomes a leader of a cell group.

We know, through experience, that the cells are the most powerful evangelistic strategy of the church. It is much easier for the cell leaders to care for those who have been reached through the people in that same cell group. This is the power of previously established, close, one on one contact. It is very important that the cells are not static. In other words, the members of a cell must not lose the spirit of evangelism and forget to invite new people.

If a cell group successfully wins one new person each week, there will be four new members added each month. Out of those four, maybe three will go to an encounter, two will go to the post-encounter, and one will go to the school of leaders. Although this is not a rule, it is an observation based on evangelistic work.

In the parable of the sower (Matthew 13:18-23), Jesus said that out of four people who receive the Word, three have trouble persevering. One will struggle with unbelief and allow Satan to rob him of the Word. Another will struggle because he wants to be a Christian without having any problems, so he'll turn away as soon as he faces his first test. And the third one struggles for worries born from the pressures of this world. Ultimately, he allows himself to be absorbed by his commitments and does not return.

Only one, out of four people, had his heart open and persevered in the whole process.

Later, he will see the positive results and be fruitful.

DILIGENCE IN CONSOLIDATION

The word that best characterizes consolidation is diligence. King Solomon said, "The desires of the diligent are fully satisfied" (Proverbs 13:4).

He also compared those who are negligent to fools, "Like cutting off one's feet of drinking violence is the sending of a message by the hand of a fool" (Proverbs 26:6).

Put another way, the leader of a cell group should not put the consolidation in the hands of a negligent person because that would be like wounding the group's legs and paralyzing them. The person in charge of consolidation is responsible to ask for the form that was filled out when the person gave his heart to the Lord, failure to do so, results in the fruit being lost.

Furthermore, the responsibility of consolidation should not be put in the hands of a shy person or someone who does not like to relate to people. The one who is responsible for consolidation should have a pastoral anointing and a fervor to care for each person. Along with these important characteristics, the person should be one who is efficient, disciplined, organized, demanding, diligent and with charisma. It takes such people to become experts in consolidating others.

INTERCESSION

Have an annual calendar of intercession. Intercession should not be relegated to specified ministries. There should be a schedule for prayer in each ministry where they not only pray for the established goals of the ministry and of the church; but at the same time, pray for the lives of the leaders and their immediate family members because in doing so they will remain within a hedge of protection.

God is looking for people to stand in the gap on behalf of others in order to stop the judgment of God and bring spiritual revival to our society. Noah's generation was completely lost because the dominant spirit, of that time which was the spirit of the world. People were turning more towards evil and sin than giving thanks to God. Only Noah and his family were saved, and that was because he made such a serious promise to God.

Abraham also interceded diligently for God to stop His judgment against Sodom and Gomorrah. The divine mandate was : "If there are ten righteous, I will not destroy the city" (Genesis 18:32). Sadly, in a society of 10,000 people, there were not even 10 righteous ones. Because of this, the judgment of God fell on them once again, and the two cities were wiped off the map. Through faith we can move the hand of God and He will use us to change the appearance of things. We can influence our city so that the favor and mercy of God can touch it and the people will become righteous and committed to Him.

REWARDS

When someone in the military is granted a medal or award for what they have done, they receive it with great appreciation, displaying such symbols of recognition in a place where everyone can see it. This brings gerat satisfaction to them and raises their self esteem. It is no different when it comes to our disciples. It blesses them when we recognize their successes, too. They are encouraged anew to keep advancing the gospel.

In the parable of the talents (Matthew 25:14-30), the Lord Jesus taught us how to reward productivity. From the negligent, he took away all responsibility, but to the most successful ones He gave even more.

In other words, if a person cannot do a good job leading a cell group, the Lord is not going to entrust that person more responsibility. But to any person who can fittingly direct a cell and make it grow, the Lord will give that person twelve cells. And for the person who properly manages those twelve cells, the Lord will provide 144 cells. And if those cells are handled well, the Lord will give to that leader 1,728 cells.

It is important that we understand that the greatest things are accomplished through the smallest details. One word of encouragement, public recognition a certificate, or a diploma can become the inspiration that motivates a leader to develop the vision for his cell and become a great blessing.

THE HARVEST IS WAITING

The promise of God is that the glory in the last days will be greater than the first. You are now living in the most favorable time for multiplication. Unprecedented growth is trekking its way around the world through the anointing of God. He wants to bring in the final harvest, but it is important for you to make a serious commitment to Him. Father, God longs to use each one of you. Just look at biblical history and you will see that very little is mentioned about the accomplishments of the architects, the engineers or lawyers, but a lot has been said about the servants of God. If you want to leave a big footprint on human history, become a servant of God who succeeds in fulfilling His purpose faithfully, reproducing himself in others. There are privileges that this world sees as amazing, but I want to tell you that no privilege, no matter how big it may be in this world, can ever be compared to being a servant of God. Solomon said that whoever wins souls is wise. Serving God has an eternal purpose. It means rescuing lives from the claws of the enemy and moving them into the kingdom of God.

Use all of your strength, all of your knowledge, all of your wisdom to rescue souls and make disciples. In order to do that, your message must be penetrating, consistent, dynamic and infused with a high level of faith.